ZOOM!

DISCOVER THE INVISIBLE WORLD OF NATURE

de

QEB
QEB Publishing

Editor: Amanda Askew
Designer: Andrew Crowson
Picture Researcher: Maria Joannou

Copyright © QEB Publishing, Inc. 2011

Published in the United States by
QEB Publishing, Inc.
3 Wrigley, Suite A
Irvine, CA 92618

www.qed-publishing.co.uk

A CIP record of this book is available from the Library of Congress.

ISBN 978 1 60992 288 7

Printed in China

▼ Flies have a short, streamlined body. They have compound eyes on the side of their head and small antennae. They eat only liquid food.

Picture credits
Alamy Images Florian Franke 86t;
Corbis Micro Discovery 39tl, Tim Pannell 60t, Carole Valkenier/All Canada Photos 65tr, Stephen Frink/Science Faction 69tr, Dr. John D. Cunningham/Visuals Unlimited 93b, Fadil 97tr, Dennis Kunkel Microscopy, Inc./Visuals Unlimited 98b;
DK Images 23tr, 36;
Flickr 86;
FLPA Mark Moffett/Minden Pictures 10b, Rolf Nussbaumer/Imagebroker 11bl, Thomas Marent/Minden Pictures 14b, Cisca Castelijns/FN/Minden Pictures 15cr, Mark Moffett/Minden Pictures 16b, Piotr Naskrecki/Minden Pictures 17b (background), Mark Moffett/Minden Pictures 18b, Murray Cooper/Minden Pictures 19b, Ingo Arndt 16b, Chien Lee/Minden Pictures 20t, Murray Cooper/Minden Pictures 21tl, Ingo Arndt 22b, Frans Lanting 23b, Michael Durham/Minden Pictures 24t, Mark Moffett/Minden Pictures 25b, Steve Trewhella 25cr, Albert Lleal/Minden Pictures 25tl, John Eveson 26–27t, Heidi & Hans-Juergen Koch/Minden Pictures 26br, Mark Moffett/Minden Pictures 27b, Gary K Smith 27t, James Christensen/Minden Pictures 28b, Albert Mans/FN/Minden 28t, Gerry Ellis/Minden Pictures 30-31, David Hosking 31bl, Mark Moffett/Minden Pictures 32cl, John Eveson 32br, Albert Mans/FN/Minden 33cl, Albert Lleal/Minden Pictures 33tl, Harri Taavetti 36b, 36-37t, Gerry Ellis/Minden Pictures 38b, Donald M. Jones 39tr, Photo Researchers 40c, Gerry Ellis/Minden Pictures 40b, John Hawkins 45b, Ingo Schulz/Imagebroker 49b, Wayne Hutchinson 51tr, Frans Lanting 51b, John Zimmermann 52l, Jim Brandenburg/Minden Pictures 52r, Jurgen & Christine Sohns 52-53, Michael & Patricia Fogden/Minden Pictures 53tr, Frans Lanting 53b, S & D & K Maslowski 55bl, Richard Costin 57tr, Jurgen & Christine Sohns 58br, Harri Taavetti 58cl, Ingo Schulz/Imagebroker 59cl, Hiroya Minakuchi/Minden Pictures 62–63, Ingo Arndt/Minden Pictures 63bl, Konrad Wothe/Minden Pictures 64l, Fred Bavendam/Minden Pictures 66–67, Chris Newbert/Minden Pictures 67t, Fred Bavendam/Minden Pictures 67b, Silvestris Fotoservice 73b, Chris Newbert/Minden Pictures 75t, Imagebroker 78bl, Hiroya Minakuchi/Minden Pictures 79b, Norbert Wu/Minden Pictures 83bl, D P Wilson 89bl, Nigel Cattlin 97b, Sunset 99tl, Albert Lleal/Minden Pictures 99tr, Nigel Cattlin 101t, Thomas Marent/Minden Pictures 102b, Michael Dietrich/Imagebroker 103b, 105b, Justus de Cuveland/Imagebroker 106b, Mark Moffett/Minden Pictures 107b, Justus de Cuveland/Imagebroker 108b, Jan Vermeer/FN/Minden 108-109, Albert Lleal/Minden Pictures 110cr, Mark Moffett/Minden Pictures 111tl, Thomas Marent/Minden Pictures 111tr;
Getty Images 87;
Nature Picture Library Nature Production 5t, Stephen Dalton 12b(2), Doug Wechsler 21b, Nature Production 25tr, Meul/ARCO 26bl, Nick Upton 29br, 31br, Stephen Dalton 31t, Doug Wechsler 33cr, NPL 34-35, Jane Burton 34b, Philippe Clement 35b, Pete Cairns 37tr, Philippe Clement 37br, Charlie Hamilton James 39b, Rolf Nussbaumer 40-41t, Mike Potts 41tr, Wegner/ARCO 45tr, Wild Wonders of Europe/Varesvu 47tr, Wild Wonders of Europe/Widstrand 47b, Jane Burton 50b (stage 2), 51cl, Pete Cairns 54l, Andy Rouse 57b, Charlie Hamilton James 58t, Wild Wonders of Europe/Widstrand 58bl, Rolf Nussbaumer 59tr, Jane Burton 59cr, Andy Rouse 59bl, NPL 60-61, Rolf Nussbaumer 60, Steve Knell 62, Jose B. Ruiz 65c, Mark Carwardine 70b, Jurgen Freund 74b, Georgette Douwma 77c, Jane Burton 78–79, David Shale 80t, 82b, 82–83, 83br, Kim Taylor 88b, 88–89t, Duncan McEwan 92-93, Ross Hoddinott 94b, 96b, Thomas Lazar 103cl, Alex Hyde 103cr, Brian Lightfoot 104bl, Nick Gordon 107tl;
Photolibrary Flirt Collection/LWA-Dann Tardif 8t, Eastphoto Eastphoto 13tl, Age Fotostock 16t, Emanuele Biggi 17tl, Antonio Lopez Roman 18c, Last Refuge 24b, Martin Ruegner 29bl, Otto Hahn 29t, Age Fotostock 32bl, Otto Hahn 33bl, Oxford Scientific/Lewis Phillips 37bl, Phototake Science 42b, Juniors Bildarchiv 44c, Phototake Science 44b, Doug Allan 54b, Tony Tilford 55t, Doug Allan 56b, Tony Tilford 59br, Animals Animals/Joyce & Frank Burek 60t, Mirko Zanni 67c, Peter Arnold Images/Jonathan Bird 72l, Peter Arnold Images/Kelvin Aitken 75b, Oxford Scientific/Paulo de Oliveira 81t, Index Stock Imagery/Henryk T. Kaiser 86b, Index Stock Imagery 100bl, Index Stock Imagery/Henryk T. Kaiser 100-101, H Stanley Johnson 104-105, 110br, Index Stock Imagery/Henryk T. Kaiser 111bl;
Photoshot NHPA/Mark Bowler 11t, NHPA/Stephen Dalton 17b, 21tr, NHPA/Nick Garbutt 41b, NHPA/M I Walker 89tr, NHPA/A.N.T. Photo Library 105t, NHPA/Laurie Campbell 108c;

Science Photo Library Tom McHugh 8b, Richard R Hansen 9b, 11br, Claude Nuridsany & Marie Perennou 12b(1), 12b(3), 12b(4), Tom McHugh 17tr, Eye of Science 22t, Tom McHugh 32cr, Steve Gschmeissner 43tl, Herve Conge, ISM 50b (stage 1), Kenneth H Thomas 51cr, Steve Gschmeissner 62b, Wim Van Egmond/Visuals Unlimited 63tr, M.I. Walker 63br, Alexander Semenov 64r, Steve Gschmeissner 65tl, Eye of Science 68t, Science Pictures Ltd 69tl, Dr. Hossler/Visuals Unlimited 69b, M.H. Sharp 70t, Alexis Rosenfeld 71b, Alexander Semenov 73tl, Kjell B.Sandved 73tr, Matthew Oldfield 74c, Peter Scoones 76t, Power and Syred 76b, Matthew Oldfield 77t, Gustav Verderber/Visuals Unlimited 78br, Wim Van Egmond/Visuals Unlimited 79t, David Wrobel/Visuals Unlimited 80b, Dr Ken MacDonald 81bl, Sinclair Stammers 83t, Power and Syred 84bl, Alexander Semenov 84br, 85tl, Jan Hinsch 87t, 7br, David Nunuk 90t, Eye of Science 90b, Dr Keith Wheeler 91tl, Steve Gschmeissner 91tr, Claude Nuridsany & Marie Perennou 91b, Eye of Science 92b, Susumu Nishinaga 93t, Adrian Thomas 94l, Merlin Tuttle 106t, Art Wolfe 107tr, Eye of Science 109b, Jan Hinsch 110tl, Steve Gschmeissner 111cr, Adrian Thomas 112; **Shutterstock** Matthew Cole 8-9, Karbunar 10-11, Studiotouch 12t, Pan Xunbin 13b, Eric Isselée 13cr, Dr. Morley Read 13tr, Chas 14-15, Pan Xunbin 15b, Alslutsky 15t, Liew Weng Keong 18-19t, Dr. Morley Read 19tr, Tischenko Irina 22-21, Matthew Cole 30b, Tischenko Irina 32t, Chas 33br, Eric Isselée 33tl, Blacqbook 34t, Frog-traveller 35t, Iv Nikolny 38t, Chris Pole 42l, MustafaNC 43tr, Nicholas Moore 43b, Joanne Harris and Daniel Bubnich 44-45, Eduardo Rivero 46l, Bernd Schmidt 46b, Dhoxax 47tl, Christian Musat 48c, Bernd Schmidt 48b, Stephen Chung 48-49, Frog-traveller 49t, Valentina_G 50t, Saied Shahin Kiya 50b (stage 3), Xavier Marchant 55br, Chris Alcock 56t, Martin Pateman 56-57, Iv Nikolny 58cr, Eduardo Rivero 59tl, Teguh Tirtaputra 60t, Cigdem Sean Cooper 70–71, Johan1900 71tr, Basel101658 92cl, Mary Lane 95tl, R McKown 95tr, Maslov Dmitry 95b, Nito 96c, Wong Hock Weng 96-97, Joseph Scott Photography 98t, Tatiana Makotra 99b, Newa 100br, Tatiana Makotra 101b, EuToch 102t, Thien Eu 103t, Calvin Chan 104br, Evlakhov Valeriy 109tr, EuToch 110bl, R McKown 110cd, Calvin Chan 111cl, Wong Hock Weng 111br, Matthew Cole 116; Loskutnikov 119.

Words in bold can be found in the Glossary on pages 112–114.

CONTENTS

OCEAN LIFE

PLANTS

ZOOM INTO...

...the world of bugs, birds, ocean life, and plants—and begin a journey that takes you to hidden places, full of mystery and surprises. With this amazing book you can imagine what it is like to be bug-sized, or what it might be like to have wings, or live under water, or even be a microscopic plant. Get ready to discover some fantastic facts and get close to the world in ways you never thought possible. It's time to ZOOM!

Zoom In

Look at an ant, a feather, a leaf, or a piece of seaweed through a microscope, or through a camera's **macro lens**, and you will notice that they appear larger than in real life. A microscope uses **lenses** to magnify the image of very small things, often several hundred times. Modern microscopes may use other techniques to magnify objects many thousands of times.

Almost Real

Pictures with the ACTUAL SIZE icons are shown at their real-life size, as though they're right on the page! Comparing things with a standard paperclip really helps you understand their size.

ACTUAL SIZE

Macro Photography

The art of taking pictures of small things in closeup is called macro photography. Using this technique, and others, photographers and scientists have helped us uncover things we never knew existed, by giving us the world in closeup. Images with the ZOOM icon show you how many times the subject has been magnified.

ZOOM x2

Try It

WHAT IS IT? images allow you to use your new investigation skills to guess what the picture might be. Just turn to page 11 to find out that IT IS…

ZOOM x3

WHAT iS it?

BUGS

READY FOR ACTION

Most bugs are small enough to hide easily. So if your survival depended on finding and catching thousands of them, you would want to be well equipped. **Mantises** have it all— great eyesight, lightning reactions, and legs covered in gripping spines.

Large eyes at the front of the head, so the mantis can judge how far away prey is.

Front legs are covered in spines to create a trap as the legs fold in on the prey.

Wait and See

Most mantises are green, so they can hide from their prey among leaves. They sit absolutely still, but they are alert and ready for action. When a mantis sees lunch approaching, it prepares for attack, and lunges in less than one thousandth of a second— that is around 300 times faster than the blink of an eye.

ZOOM x9

Praying mantis

ZOOM x3

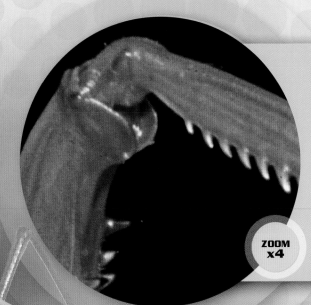

ZOOM x4

Poised for Action
The mantis's front legs are bent, and held in a strange position that makes it look as if it is praying. In reality, these spiked legs are ready for a much less peaceful activity. Fast and strong, the vice-like limbs can catch and crush an insect in less than a second.

While the front half of the body lunges forward, the back half stays still.

FACTOID

Some mantises are big enough to hunt for larger prey. They can attack birds and lizards.

VITAL STATISTICS

Common name	Praying mantis
Latin name	*Mantidae*
Size	6 in (15 cm) in length
Habitat	Forests
Special feature	Lightning-fast predator

Leafy insects
*This giant leaf insect has **camouflaged** itself by pretending to be part of a plant. When an animal pretends to be something else, it is called a mimic. Look closely to see this bug has fake 'veins' and brown edges, just like a real leaf.*

GROWING UP

Look deep into the world of bugs and you will find that incredible changes take place as their **lifecycles** unfold. Take an ugly blowfly as an example. With its large eyes, bristly body, and shiny green **cuticle**, this fly is easy to recognize. But would you recognize its young so easily?

◀ Blowflies with a green, metallic sheen are called greenbottles.

ZOOM
x 14

All Change

*Most bugs begin life looking completely different from the way they will look as adults. They go through extraordinary changes as they grow. Each change is a **metamorphosis**— which means "transform shape."*

The Blowfly's Lifecycle

1 A female blowfly can smell a dead body, open wound, or meat. Within minutes, she arrives to lay around 250 eggs on it. Just 24 hours later, each egg hatches into a tiny **grub**, called a maggot or **larva**.

2 The maggots feed on the flesh or food and as they grow, they **molt**. After two molts, the maggots are much larger and will soon be ready to metamorphose.

3 Each maggot grows a tough, dark case around its body and becomes a **pupa**.

4 It takes at least six days for the pupa to transform into an adult. When the pupa breaks open, an adult blowfly emerges.

Silky Case

Some bugs wrap themselves in a silk **cocoon** when they pupate. They make the silk in special silk glands in their bodies. The larvae of silkworm moths are kept in large farms, and the silk from their cocoons is used to weave silk for clothing.

Stripping Off

When a bug grows, it gets too large for its tough skin, or cuticle. The simple solution is to strip off the old skin— this is called molting— to reveal a new, larger cuticle underneath.

ZOOM x 12

ACTUAL SIZE

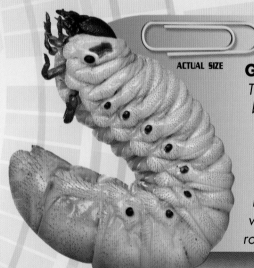

Giant Grubs

The larva of a Hercules beetle can reach up to 6 inches (15 centimeters) long and weigh 5 ounces (150 grams), making it one of the largest grubs in the world. It feeds on soft, rotting wood.

WHAT IS IT?

ZOOM x 160

BIG-EYED BUGS

How great would your eyesight be if your eyes covered your whole head? Members of the dragonfly family are lucky enough to have enormous eyes and great vision. Their eyesight is so good, these insects can see in almost every direction. They can see colors (except red) and even **ultraviolet** light, which is a type of light that humans cannot see.

With thousands of lenses in each eye, the dragonfly can spot the slightest movement.

Like all insects, the dragonfly has six legs.

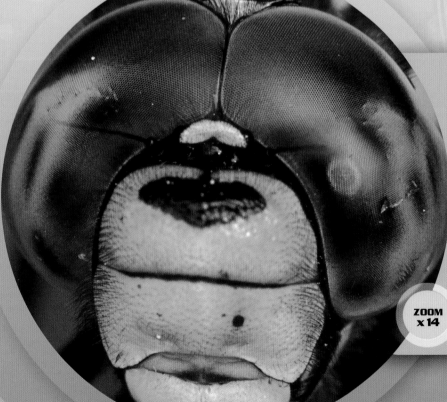

ZOOM x 14

A Trick of the Light

The Southern Hawker dragonfly has 30,000 lenses in each eye. A lens focuses light that enters the eyes, and nerves carry the image to the brain. The brain takes all 60,000 images and turns them into a fantastic ability to see. Insect eyes are especially good at detecting movement. Human eyes have just one lens each— but the quality of images that our brains can see is much better.

Strong, transparent wings make this insect a powerful flier.

Air Acrobatics
Members of the dragonfly family aren't just superb at seeing, they are also among the world's best fliers. They can twist and turn each of their long, lacy wings independently, so they can fly forward, backward, change direction quickly, and even hover.

ZOOM x13

Elongated body

Dragonfly

ZOOM x5

FACTOID

Prehistoric dragonflies were enormous, with a wingspan of 30 inches (75 centimeters)!

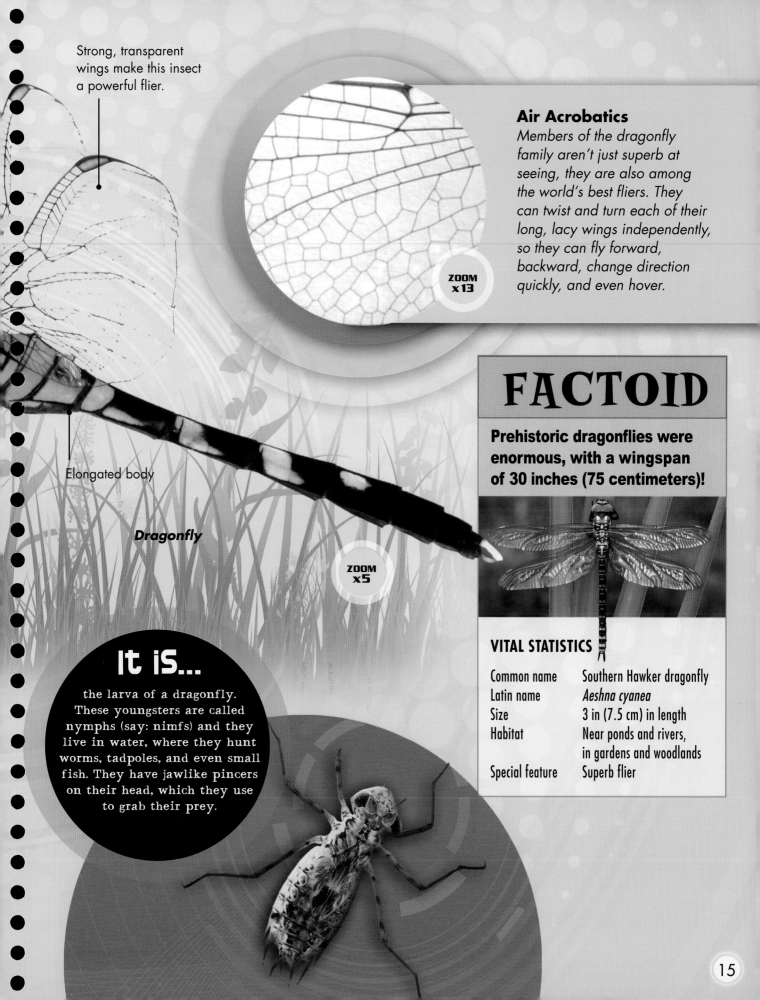

VITAL STATISTICS

Common name	Southern Hawker dragonfly
Latin name	*Aeshna cyanea*
Size	3 in (7.5 cm) in length
Habitat	Near ponds and rivers, in gardens and woodlands
Special feature	Superb flier

It is...

the larva of a dragonfly. These youngsters are called nymphs (say: nimfs) and they live in water, where they hunt worms, tadpoles, and even small fish. They have jawlike pincers on their head, which they use to grab their prey.

JAWS AND CLAWS

Down in the dark, murky world of bugs, there is a war going on! Even easygoing plant eaters need weapons to defend themselves. Mouthparts often have to do two jobs—killing and eating. Jaws and claws come in all shapes and sizes, each one best suited to that particular bug's lifestyle.

◄ Camel spiders can reach up to 6 inches (15 centimeters) in length. They have two powerful pincers attached to the front of their massive jaws.

Giant Jaws
Camel spiders are equipped for battle. Their jaws are up to one-third of the size of their entire body. They use them to fight predators, or to grab prey, such as lizards. Then they pour **digestive juices** *over their prey before digging in.*

WHAT IS IT?

ZOOM x20

Sticky Claws and Sucking Straws

Assassin bugs use their powerful, sticky legs to grab hold of another insect. They stick a tube-shaped mouthpart into their prey, and pour digestive juices into it. This turns the prey's insides into a thick liquid, which the bug sucks up.

ZOOM
x2

Creepy Crawly

Centipedes are best known for having lots of legs, but they use one pair as deadly claws. The front pair of legs has evolved into nasty, sharp claws that can inject deadly **venom** into predators or prey.

ACTUAL SIZE

Mighty Munchers

A plague of locusts can cause chaos. Their enormous **mandibles**—the chewing and crushing mouthparts—are so strong and fast that a locust can eat its body weight in food in just one day. A swarm of locusts can be 460 square miles (1,200 square kilometers) in size—the size of a large city—and it can contain 80 million locusts. One swarm can wolf down 420 million pounds (190 million kilograms) of plants in a day.

ANTS UNITED

The menacing face of an ant hides a brilliant brain. These little bugs have larger brains than any other insect, with 250,000 brain **cells** each. Their real intelligence, however, comes from the way ants work together. Scientists think that a **colony** of ants operates like a super-brain. A colony can make decisions, working together in the same way that the cells inside our brains coordinate their efforts.

Driver ant

ZOOM x15

Hooked claws help the ant climb over plants.

Ready for Action

Ants have two main eyes, which can detect movement, and three smaller eyes, called ocelli, which are better at detecting levels of light. Their main sense, however, is smell. Strong jaws, or mandibles, can be used to tear and carry food, build nests, or bite prey.

ZOOM x22

It is...

a queen herdsman ant, leading her colony to a new nest. From time to time, a queen decides to lead her whole colony nearer to food supplies, and a new nest is built. The colony may contain more than 10,000 workers and 4,000 larvae and pupae.

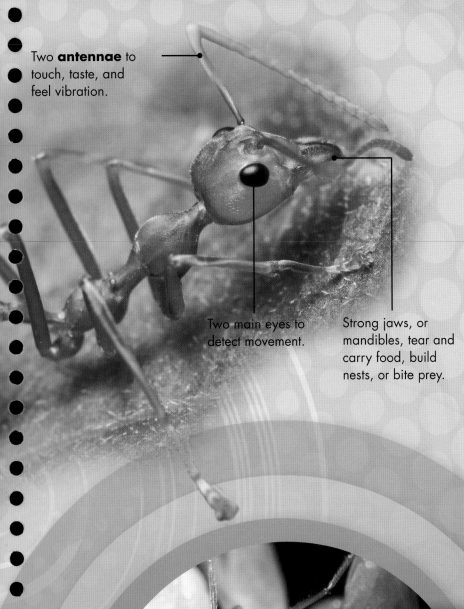

Two **antennae** to touch, taste, and feel vibration.

Two main eyes to detect movement.

Strong jaws, or mandibles, tear and carry food, build nests, or bite prey.

FACTOID

Driver ants are the largest ants in the world. Working together, a colony attacks every animal in its path—including snakes and people.

VITAL STATISTICS

Common name	Driver ant
Latin name	*Dorylus nigricans*
Size	2 in (5 cm) in length
Habitat	Rain forests and grasslands
Special feature	Can live in colonies of 20 million ants

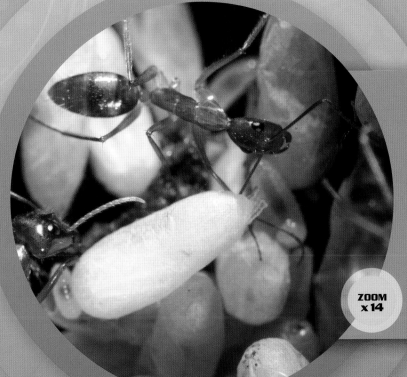

ZOOM x14

Job Share

Ants are called social insects because they live and work together. One queen lays all the colony's eggs. Worker ants are wingless females (left) that do all the chores, including fetching food, nest-building, and taking care of the eggs. Male ants grow wings and create swarms at mating time.

HIDDEN FROM VIEW

Even with the best camera equipment, or the sharpest eyesight, it can be almost impossible to find some bugs. Look closely at these pictures and be amazed at the many ways nature uses color, pattern, and shape to make an animal disappear from view.

◄ A **katydid**'s camouflage makes it blend into the tree bark, so it isn't seen by prey or predators.

ZOOM x3.5

Singing for Your Mate
When a bug is cunningly disguised as a leaf or patch of moss, how can it expect its mates to find it? One answer is to sing. Katydids are bush crickets that are masters of deception, but they alert mates to their presence with a loud and characteristic song that sounds like "katy-she-did."

WHAT IS IT?

ZOOM x2

Prickly Problems

When treehoppers suck the tasty sap from inside a plant stem, they become easy targets for predators. They overcome this problem by disguising themselves as part of the plant. The young bugs look like the brown, knobbly bark, but the adults pretend they are prickly green thorns instead.

Pretty as a Petal

Colorful crab spiders perch motionless on flowers, and calmly wait for lunch to walk by. These lurking predators are invisible because their colors are flawlessly matched to the colors of the petals.

ZOOM
x5

ZOOM
x 10

Clever Tricks

This trickery certainly works on birds, which normally wouldn't hesitate to swoop down and pluck a fat, juicy caterpillar from its feeding grounds. With a green body, the caterpillar is camouflaged among leaves, but that freaky face on the caterpillar's rear end is enough to make any sharp-eyed predator think twice.

ZOOM
x2

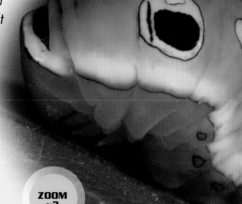

BEAUTIFUL BUGS

Have you ever wondered how butterflies are able to produce such dramatic colors and patterns on their wings? The secret lies in the structure of tiny scales that are able to turn light into incredibly vivid blues, reds, and greens. Some butterflies even appear to have a metallic sheen to their wings.

Creating Color

*The overlapping scales on a butterfly's wing can have a range of color **pigments**, shiny reflective "mirrors," and air spaces. These work together to absorb ultraviolet light, which our eyes can't see, and turn it into bright patches of blue and green. They work in a similar way to light-emitting diodes (LEDs), which are used in televisions.*

ZOOM x700

Iridescent colors on a butterfly's wings change depending on the angle from which you view them.

It is...

an owl butterfly, flaunting its eerie-looking **eyespot**. The flash of the "eye," when the butterfly flutters its wings, is startling, and might make a predator think twice before attacking...all the time the butterfly needs to make its escape.

The **proboscis**, or mouthpart, is shaped like a straw, but absorbs liquid.

Peacock butterfly

ZOOM x3

ZOOM x5

Short but Sweet

The larvae of butterflies and moths are called caterpillars, and their job is to feed and grow. This caterpillar's stunning skin is a colorful warning that it is covered with stinging bristles. After metamorphosis this impressive little beast will emerge from a cocoon as a drab brown moth.

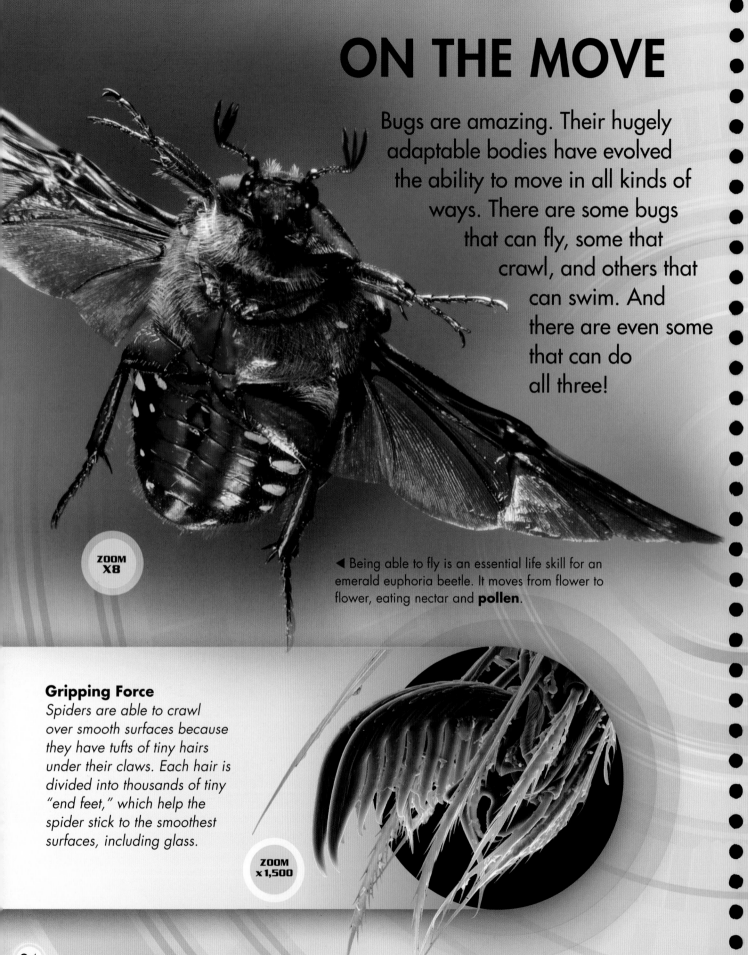

ON THE MOVE

Bugs are amazing. Their hugely adaptable bodies have evolved the ability to move in all kinds of ways. There are some bugs that can fly, some that crawl, and others that can swim. And there are even some that can do all three!

ZOOM X8

◀ Being able to fly is an essential life skill for an emerald euphoria beetle. It moves from flower to flower, eating nectar and **pollen**.

Gripping Force

Spiders are able to crawl over smooth surfaces because they have tufts of tiny hairs under their claws. Each hair is divided into thousands of tiny "end feet," which help the spider stick to the smoothest surfaces, including glass.

ZOOM x 1,500

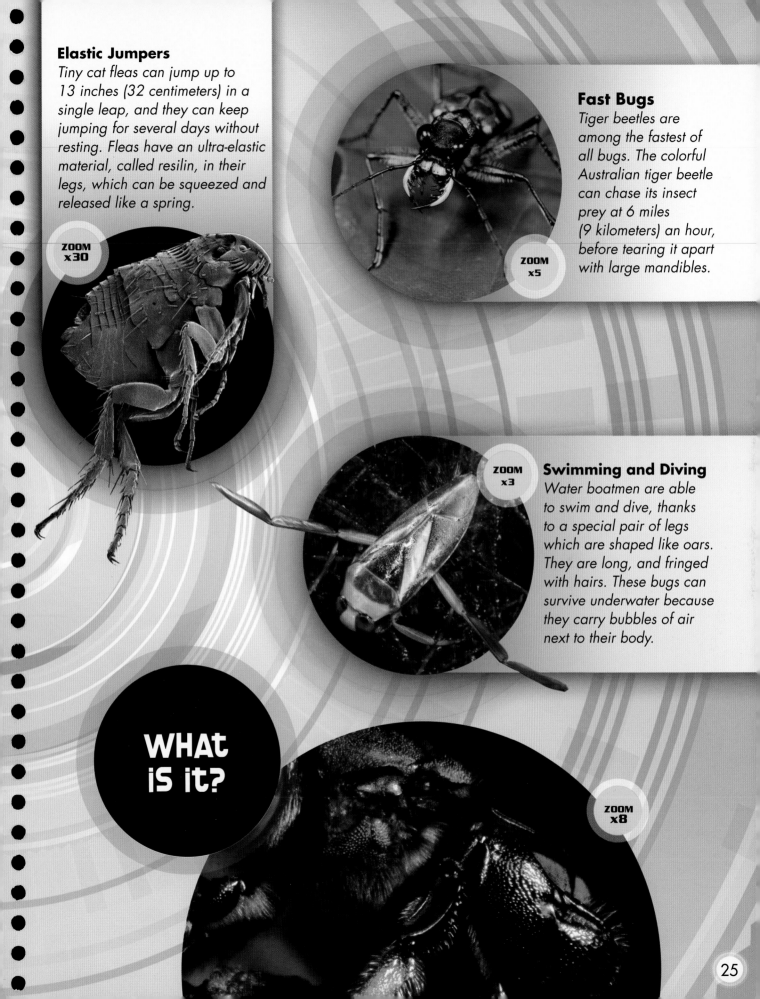

Elastic Jumpers

Tiny cat fleas can jump up to 13 inches (32 centimeters) in a single leap, and they can keep jumping for several days without resting. Fleas have an ultra-elastic material, called resilin, in their legs, which can be squeezed and released like a spring.

ZOOM x30

Fast Bugs

Tiger beetles are among the fastest of all bugs. The colorful Australian tiger beetle can chase its insect prey at 6 miles (9 kilometers) an hour, before tearing it apart with large mandibles.

ZOOM x5

Swimming and Diving

Water boatmen are able to swim and dive, thanks to a special pair of legs which are shaped like oars. They are long, and fringed with hairs. These bugs can survive underwater because they carry bubbles of air next to their body.

ZOOM x3

WHAT IS IT?

ZOOM x8

HONEY MONSTERS

Most of us think twice before getting up close and personal to a bee. That buzzing sound, those warning stripes, and the fear of being stung are all good ways to keep us—and predators—at arms' length. In fact, bees are among the most important bugs on the planet. Without them, flowers would not grow **seeds**, and we would quickly run out of food.

The chest area, or thorax, is packed with muscles used for flying.

FACTOID

Bees travel 56,000 miles (90,000 kilometers), and visit more than two million flowers, to make a single pot of honey. One honeybee will produce just half a teaspoon of honey in its whole life.

VITAL STATISTICS

Common name	Honeybee
Latin name	*Apis mellifera*
Size	1 in (2.5 cm) in length
Habitat	Any place where flowers grow
Special feature	Can turn nectar and pollen from flowers into sweet honey

ZOOM x5

Super Storage
Bees have pollen baskets on their legs, which they use to store pollen that they collect from flowers. Worker bees use the pollen to make honey, and to feed the colony.

The legs are covered in small hairs. Pollen sticks to them.

Bee

Sting for protection (females only). If it uses the sting, it will die.

ZOOM x8

Four wings

Home Sweet Home

A beehive is home to the colony. The queen lays eggs in wax cells, where they are tended by workers. When the eggs hatch, workers feed the larvae. Most of the larvae will grow into workers. Some of them will grow into males, which are called drones. A few will grow into queens.

ZOOM x2

It is...

an orchid bee. These are the only animals, apart from humans, that are known to make perfumes. Males collect scents from orchid flowers and mix them with other ingredients, such as fruit, to make a perfume that attracts females.

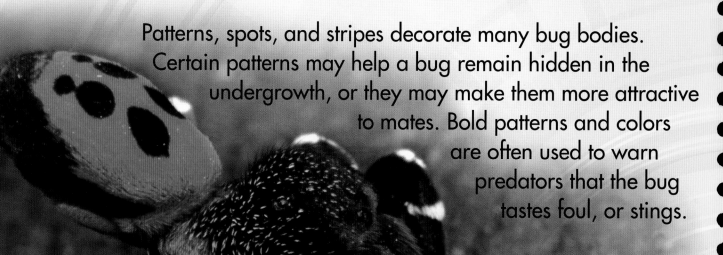

SPOTS AND STRIPES

Patterns, spots, and stripes decorate many bug bodies. Certain patterns may help a bug remain hidden in the undergrowth, or they may make them more attractive to mates. Bold patterns and colors are often used to warn predators that the bug tastes foul, or stings.

ZOOM x20

Dressed to Impress
*Glamorous male ladybug spiders use their red back, black spots, and white-banded legs to impress females, who are dark and dull by comparison. Each female can lay only one **brood** of eggs because when they hatch, the little **spiderlings** gang up and eat her!*

Pretty in Peach
Velvet worms have delicate colors, and often patterns, on their soft, squidgy body. These animals live in dark, moist habitats and can shoot a jet of slime to catch their prey.

ZOOM x2

ZOOM x4

Spiral Puzzle

Grove snails with light-colored shells live in warmer places than those with dark shells. No one knows why some grove snails have dark spiral bands while others have plain shells.

WHAT IS it?

ZOOM x10

Blue Genes

*How do bugs create colors and patterns on their bodies? Scientists think it might be the work of a special **protein** called morphogen. When morphogen reaches certain parts of the bug's body, it tells them to start making pigment, which creates color. It is the bug's **genes** that decide where the morphogen will have this effect.*

ZOOM x14

29

HAIRY NOT SCARY

Tarantula

ACTUAL SIZE

Imagine you could shrink to the size of a bird-eating spider, and come face to face with one of these mini-beasts. These are the largest of all spiders, and some of the biggest bugs on the planet. Fortunately, bird-eating spiders—also known as tarantulas—look deadlier than they really are.

Eight eyes—some to detect light and some to detect movement.

Leglike limbs, called pedipalps, are used for touch and to hold prey.

Fangs, called chelicerae, inject venom into prey.

A Bad Rep
Lots of people are afraid of spiders, but they don't deserve their bad reputation. Very few spiders are capable of hurting humans, and spider bites are very rare events. In fact, spiders are incredibly important. They kill flies and other disease-bearing bugs, and are food for billions of other animals, including mammals, birds, reptiles, and amphibians.

Spiky hairs on the back

ZOOM x2

Touchy-feely

Spiders have little hairs all over their body. The hairs are essential to a spider's survival. They are extremely sensitive to touch and vibration, so they alert the spider to the presence of another animal nearby. Even blind spiders, such as those that live in caves, can find and catch a fly, just by using this kind of information.

Four pairs of legs

FACTOID

Spiders do not have a tongue or a nose. They can smell and taste things by using the special hairs on their legs.

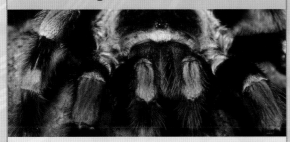

VITAL STATISTICS

Common name	Mexican redknee tarantula
Latin name	*Brachypelma smithi*
Size	7 in (18 cm) in length
Habitat	Scrubland and deserts
Special feature	Can live for more than 20 years

It is...

a female wasp spider, with bright warning stripes. Males are small, brown, and easy to miss. These spiders are orb weavers, which means they create complex webs of silk. They use the webs to catch their prey, which are killed with a venomous bite.

USE YOUR EYES

Study these zooms that appear throughout the chapter. Can you recognize any of them just by looking at them? Are there any clues, such as color, body parts, or shape, that help you work out where you've seen these images before?

1 As I flutter by you will see flashes of vibrant color.

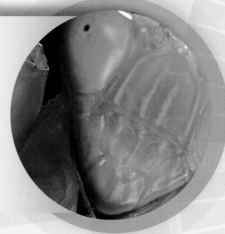

2 I pray for my dinner, but beware my striking pose. Who am I?

3 I am a giant Scolopendran, but you know me better by my common name.

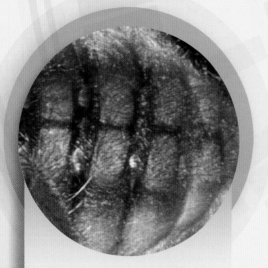

4 I am a desert fighter with mighty mandibles.

5 I am the sweetest of bugs with a sting in the tail.

6 Cats might think I am an irritating pest.

7 I spend all my time eating and growing. When I grow up, I want to be a giant beetle, with legs and wings.

8 My name could fool you. I'm no lady and I have eight legs, not six (or even two!).

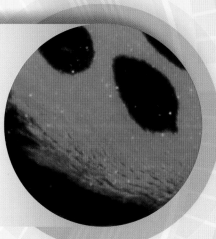

9 Who are you looking at? This giant eye is a clever trick.

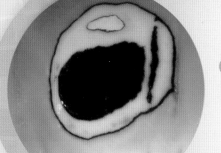

10 You could get dizzy following my lovely spiral.

11 My eyes are larger than my brain but are you smart enough to name me?

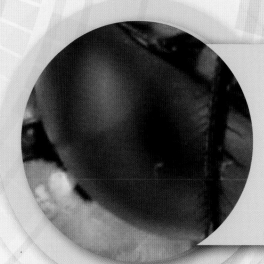

Answers: 1. p23 2. p10 3. p17 4. p16 5. p26 6. p25 7. p13 8. p28 9. p21 10. p29 11. p14

BIRDS

SILENT BUT DEADLY

The feathers on an owl's face help focus sound toward its ears.

Owl

Owls are the silent hunters of the night. Under cover of darkness they swoop through the forest, searching for small animals to eat. With superb eyesight, they can spot the smallest movement and quietly move in for the kill.

Eyes to the Front

While most birds have eyes on the sides of their head, owls have eyes that face forward. Forward-facing eyes are better for focusing on prey, to judge both distance and the speed of movement.

ACTUAL SIZE

These owls fly with soft, slow wingbeats, often close to the ground.

The bill is usually hooked and sharp for tearing at meat.

Feathers are often colored to provide camouflage.

Softly, Softly

*Owls have soft **downy** feathers on their body and feet. These help to muffle the noise of their wings in flight, which means they can approach their prey in silence. Feathers around their ears help direct sound right into the ear canal.*

ACTUAL SIZE

FACTOID

Eurasian eagle owls are huge, with a wingspan of 6 feet (2 meters). They prey on foxes, small deer, and other large owls.

VITAL STATISTICS

Common name	Eurasian eagle owl
Latin name	*Bupo bupo*
Size	28 in (70 cm) in length
Habitat	Forests, grasslands, and deserts
Special feature	Calls "ooho-oohu-oohu"

Owl Pellets

Owls can't digest all the bones, claws, fur, and teeth they swallow. These hard pieces are collected in part of the bird's stomach, then brought up and coughed out of the mouth as a pellet.

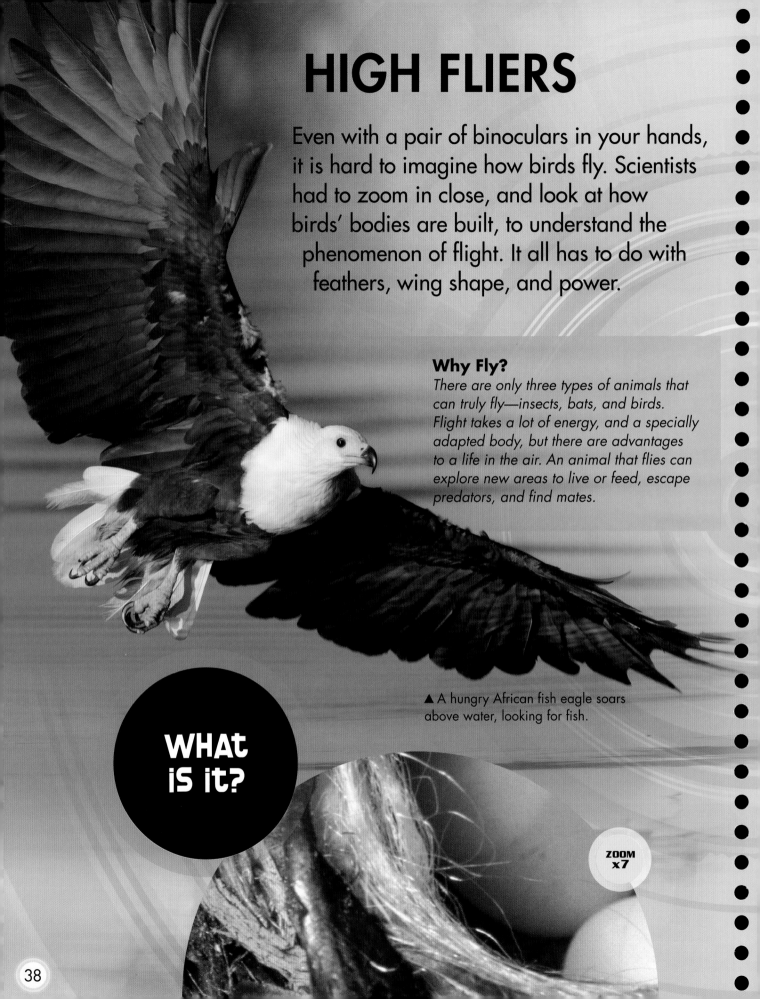

HIGH FLIERS

Even with a pair of binoculars in your hands, it is hard to imagine how birds fly. Scientists had to zoom in close, and look at how birds' bodies are built, to understand the phenomenon of flight. It all has to do with feathers, wing shape, and power.

Why Fly?

There are only three types of animals that can truly fly—insects, bats, and birds. Flight takes a lot of energy, and a specially adapted body, but there are advantages to a life in the air. An animal that flies can explore new areas to live or feed, escape predators, and find mates.

▲ A hungry African fish eagle soars above water, looking for fish.

WHAT IS it?

ZOOM x7

Holey Bones

Bones can be heavy, so to save weight—and energy—birds have bones that are filled with air. The struts, or bars, of bone keep the structure strong but very light.

ZOOM x25

Flap and Lift

Birds need two forces to fly: lift, which raises them off the ground; and thrust, which pushes the bird forward. They achieve this by flapping their wings. These limbs are shaped so air moves over the top and bottom at different speeds, which helps lift the bird up and then move it forward.

Ways to Fly

Birds change the way they move their wings and their flapping speed to fly, soar, accelerate, or swoop. When a kingfisher dives into water, its eyes are focused upon a fish. It spreads its wing and tail feathers to slow down as it enters the water. With a fish in its bill, the kingfisher will shoot out of the water and fly to a tree to devour its prey.

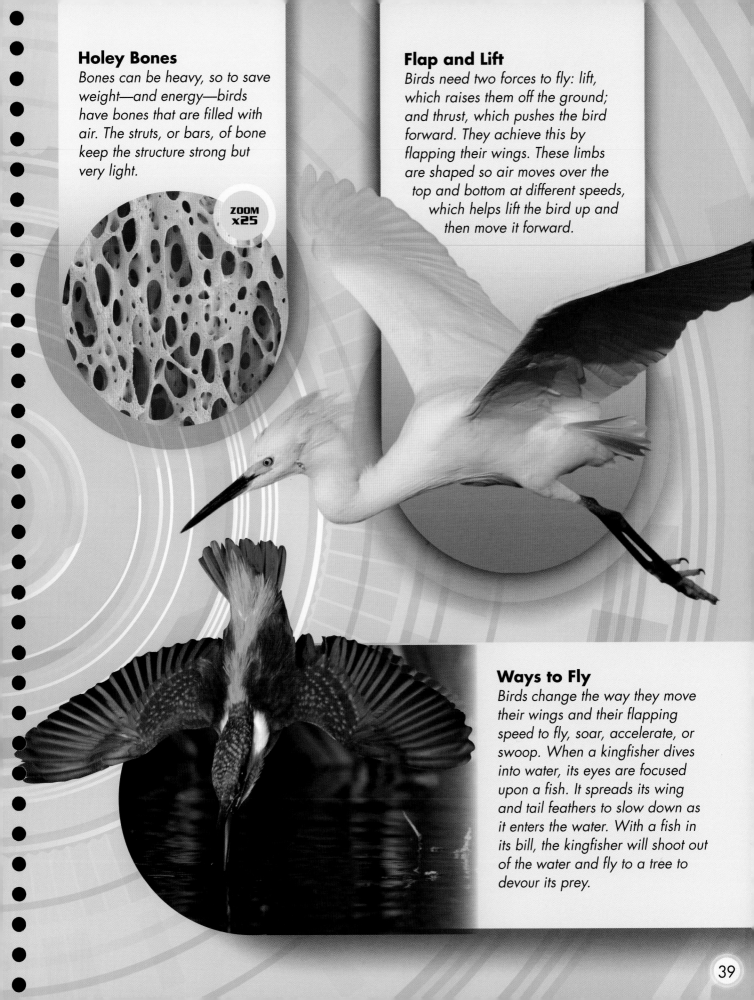

SPEEDY WINGS

Little hummingbirds are like flying gems of the forest. They zip and dart through the air, visiting up to 2,000 **tropical** flowers a day to feed at lightning speed. This way of life is so exhausting that hummingbirds spend most of their time sleeping or resting!

Beating its wings 50 times every single minute enables the bird to hover, but it burns energy fast.

Air Acrobats

These birds can feed at flowers by hovering—flying while staying in one place. Hummingbirds achieve this incredible feat by moving their wings in a figure-of-eight rather than flapping them up and down.

ACTUAL SIZE

It is...

a hummingbird nest. These little birds lay the smallest eggs, some no bigger than a pea. The nests and eggs of some hummingbirds are so small and well hidden that they have never been found.

ZOOM x2

Long, slender bill to reach deep into a flower and get nectar.

Both male and female hummingbirds usually have bright, colorful plumage.

A small body and active life mean this hummingbird must feed on an energy-rich food source: sugary nectar.

Tiny bee hummingbirds are the smallest birds in the world, with an average wingspan of just one inch (2.5 centimeters).

VITAL STATISTICS

Common name	Bee hummingbird
Latin name	*Mellisuga helenae*
Size	2.5 in (6 cm) in length
Habitat	Tropical forests
Special feature	Females lay two pea-sized eggs

Rainbow Colors

Hummingbird feathers have a beautiful metallic shimmer, which is called iridescence. The colors are created when light hits the feathers and is bent, or refracted, back in the same way that colors form in the thin film of a soap bubble.

ZOOM x 10

FINE FEATHERS

Feathers are special structures that have extraordinary properties. They keep birds dry, warm, or cool—and are essential for flight. Feathers are made of **keratin**, which is the same protein you have in your nails and hair.

◄ Male and female gray crowned cranes wear splendid **crests** of stiff gold feathers.

ACTUAL SIZE

Pretty Plumage
A bird's feathers are called its plumage and the colors are a balance between camouflage and attention-seeking. Birds that need to hide from predators often have dull brown plumage. Others—often male birds—like to show off with fine feathers, bold colors, and impressive crests or tails.

ZOOM x 120

WHAT IS IT?

Zoom a Plume

A powerful microscope, called a scanning electron microscope, reveals the incredible structure of a penguin's feather. Orange **barbs** fan out from a central shaft, or **rachis**. Each barb has many tiny hooked filaments, called **barbules**. They hook together, trapping air to keep the bird warm, and help make its plumage waterproof.

ZOOM x100

Feather Types

A bird's large, stiff feathers are mostly used for flight, and are found on its wings and tail. Contour feathers, like this one, grow over the bird's body. The barbs overlap, and help give a bird its streamlined shape. Soft, downy **plumes** near the base of the feather's rachis trap air and insulate the body (keep it warm by preventing the escape of the bird's body heat).

ZOOM x3

Fit for Flight

Flight feathers are called ramiges. Primary flight feathers, like these, grow on the wingtips and can be spread out to give the wing a large surface area. A bird can fan out its ramiges, or twist them, to control the direction and speed of flight. Like ramiges, a bird's tail feathers are stiff and can be moved. By dipping and spreading its tail feathers, a bird can rapidly slow down to avoid a crash-landing.

FABULOUS FINCH

Gouldian finches have such colorful feathers, they look as if they have been dipped in paint. These birds live only in parts of northern Australia, where they were once common. Now Gouldian finches are rare and fewer than 250 live in the wild.

Stout, strong bill for cracking open seeds.

Black, red, or orange-yellow face

Drab Chicks

Gouldian finches may stay with the same mate for life. The chicks have a drab plumage compared with their parents. Until they can leave the nest, the chicks are vulnerable to predators. Flashy feathers would be like wearing an "Eat me" sign!

ACTUAL SIZE

Gouldian finch

ZOOM x2

It is...

a bird feather louse, a type of parasite, nestled between feather barbs. Some bird parasites eat feathers; others suck blood. Gouldian finches suffer from burrowing mite parasites, which feed on their skin.

Brightly colored plumage

Males have longer tails than females.

FACTOID

Sixty years ago, there were millions of Gouldian finches. They are so rare because many have been captured to be kept in cages, and their forest habitat has been destroyed.

VITAL STATISTICS

Common name	Gouldian finch
Latin name	*Erythrura gouldiae*
Size	5 in (13 cm) in length
Habitat	Grasslands and forests
Special feature	Incredible colors

Handsome Hawfinch

The plumage of this male hawfinch will impress any females nearby. These finches live in cooler places than Gouldian finches, and balance the need for fine feathers with an ability to hide from predators in dense woodlands. Their tough bills can break open olive and cherry pits.

ZOOM x2

IT FITS THE BILL

When you look closely at a bird, pay particular attention to the shape and size of its bill. This tough, toothless mouth can tell you more about how the bird lives its life than any other body part. A bill grows from a bird's skull, and it keeps growing throughout a bird's life. It is constantly worn away, so it doesn't get any larger in an adult bird.

ACTUAL SIZE

Big Mouth

Toucans have huge, colorful bills. These tropical birds don't need large bills for their diet of fruit and insects, so why carry around such big mouths? No one knows, although a large bill may work like a giant air-conditioning unit, helping the birds to stay cool.

ZOOM x4

WHAT IS IT?

Small but Strong

Cone-shaped bills are particularly strong near the base. They are the perfect shape for tackling hard nuts, and getting through a tough skin and into the soft flesh of a fruit. This greenfinch uses its cone-shaped bill to crack open sunflower seeds.

Keeping a Safe Distance

Birds that eat insects often have tweezer-like bills. The bills are often long, to keep a bird safe from stings or bites. Bee-eaters grab their prey in their bill, and then hit them against a branch until they have released their sting.

Table Manners

Birds of prey, such as this white-tailed eagle, tear at meat. These huge birds **scavenge**, which means they feed on dying or dead animals. A long bill helps keep bacteria and blood away from their feathers, eyes, and nostrils.

BRILLIANT BIRDS

African gray parrots are super-smart birds. In fact, some people think that they are as intelligent as whales, apes, and even young children! Parrots are noisy, colorful birds that live in large groups, or colonies.

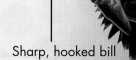

Bare skin around yellow eye

Sharp, hooked bill

Unusual Feeding

Parrots, such as this scarlet macaw, use their feet like hands, grabbing hold of food to bring it up to their mouth. Blue hyacinth macaws eat tough palm nuts. They often pick nuts out of cow dung because they are easier to eat after they have been through a cow's digestive system!

ACTUAL SIZE

It is...

a hill mynah. These glossy birds are famous for their ability to mimic, or copy, human voices. Parrots do not just mimic; they can learn the meaning of some words.

Light Fantastic

The colors of parrot feathers are unique, and are created in a way shared by no other birds. Parrot feathers scatter light, and contain unusual pigments (substances that create color) to produce vivid blues, greens, and reds.

ACTUAL SIZE

Gray feathers with white edges

FACTOID

Members of the parrot family can live long lives—up to 80 years. However, this group of birds is threatened with extinction.

VITAL STATISTICS

Common name	African gray parrot
Latin name	*Psittacus erithacus*
Size	13 in (33 cm) in length
Habitat	Lowland tropical forest
Special feature	Talkative

Gray parrot

Adults are not as colorful as many other parrots, but they do have cherry-red tail feathers.

49

THE MIRACLE OF AN EGG

Female birds lay eggs, and most parent birds look after their chicks as they grow. If you could look inside an egg and watch a chick develop, you would observe one of nature's most incredible events.

ACTUAL SIZE

◀ It took about 21 days for this baby chicken to develop inside its egg. Smaller birds, such as sparrows, can hatch in less than two weeks.

A Chick's Lifecycle

1 **Membranes** keep liquids in the egg and allow gases to pass through the shell. The yellow yolk contains food for the growing chick.

2 The shell gets thinner as the chick grows. The calcium it contains is used to build the chick's skeleton. Eggwhite (albumen) protects the chick, and provides food.

3 Chicks have a small "tooth" on their bill, which they use to crack open the shell.

4 A newly hatched chick has damp feathers, but they soon dry to become soft and fluffy.

Grow Zone

Eggs contain all the food a growing chick will need before it hatches. However, the chicks must be kept warm to develop. This means the parents have to sit on the eggs—it is a process called incubation.

ACTUAL SIZE

Hens Lay Eggs

All female birds are called hens, not just chickens. The eggs are developing inside the body even before the hens mate with the male birds. The male birds **fertilize** the eggs during mating.

Feed Me!

Chicks can open their large mouths extra wide. They rely on their parents to bring food to them while they grow. When they are ready to fly, they are called fledglings.

ZOOM x4

WHAT IS IT?

ACTUAL SIZE

BUILDING MARVELS

Weavers are the best builders in the bird world. They build the most extraordinary nests. If you look closely, you will see that they don't just pile pieces of plants on top of each other—they actually weave them together to create an elaborate and strong fortress.

Grasses or reeds are woven together to create the nest walls.

ZOOM x2

Mud and Spit
Swallows build their nests with mud and spit, then line it with soft straw and feathers. Tucked up in their cup-shaped nest, these barn swallow chicks can feed and grow, while staying out of danger from predators.

FACTOID

Cape weavers sometimes build nests that hang from branches above water, where few predators can reach them. But if the water level rises, the nests will flood and the chicks will drown.

VITAL STATISTICS

Common name	Cape weaver
Latin name	*Ploceus capensis*
Size	7 in (18 cm) in length
Habitat	Woodlands
Special feature	Superb nest-builders

The nest entrance is usually a tunnel.

Watch Me!
Male satin bowerbirds decorate their bowers with any blue or yellow objects they can find. The bower is like a stage, where the males dance and display for females.

The male builds the nest, then sings and dances to attract females to inspect his handiwork.

Weaver bird

It is...
an Emperor penguin chick. There are no nest-building materials in its Antarctic home, so the parents hold the egg, and then the chick, on their feet to keep it warm.

The nest is built between two supports, such as branches or thick grass stems.

PERCH, WALK, AND WADE

You can tell a lot about a bird by looking at its feet. Just as a closeup view of a bird's bill will give you clues about its diet, zooming in on a bird's lower limbs will tell you something about where, and how, it lives.

◄ A closeup of a white-tailed eagle as it swoops in for the kill reveals the power of this mighty predator.

Nonslip Feet

Birds of prey grab hold of squirming creatures, so they need strong, clawed **talons** *to grip tightly. White-tailed eagles pluck slippery fish out of the water but they are also equipped to hunt mammals and other birds, and to scavenge.*

WHAT IS IT?

ZOOM x2

ACTUAL SIZE

Waterbirds

Birds, such as coots, that wade through shallow water looking for small animals to eat often have long, slender legs. Their feet have long toes that are spread far apart, to keep the bird from sinking into mud. Swimming birds, such as ducks and penguins, have webbed feet. Webbing helps them move through the water with speed and power.

ZOOM x2

Sleep Tight

Perching birds, or passerines, have three toes pointing forward on each foot, and one toe pointing backward. This arrangement means a passerine can grip tightly on to a branch, even when it is sleeping.

Big Kickers

Ostriches are huge birds that can run at speeds of 45 miles (70 kilometers) an hour, but cannot fly. They have just two large, fat toes on each foot and can kick with enough force to kill a lion.

HUNTERS BY THE OCEAN

Puffins are one of the world's strangest-looking birds. They have been called "sea parrots" and "clowns of the ocean" because of their comical face and colored bill. These striking seabirds are not great fliers, but their swimming and hunting skills are awesome.

Gray or white face

Strong, conical bill

Puffin

Brightly colored bill in summer —with blue, red, and yellow parts.

ZOOM x2

All at Sea

Puffins are fearless swimmers in the open oceans, paddling with their large, orange-webbed feet. They can dive deep below the surface, as far as 65 feet (20 meters), in pursuit of prey, and can stay there for up to 30 seconds at a time.

It is...

the egg of a guillemot. These seabirds lay their eggs directly onto a bare cliff edge, with no nest to protect them. The unusual shape of the egg keeps it from rolling off.

Unusual red and black eye markings

VITAL STATISTICS

Common name	Atlantic puffin
Latin name	*Fratercula arctica*
Size	12 in (30 cm) in length
Habitat	Sea cliffs and open seas
Special feature	Feed in large groups called rafts

A white breast and a black body

Ferrying Fish

Once a puffin has reached its prey—usually small fish—it can catch and hold several at a time. It does this by pushing a fish up with its tongue, onto spikes on the roof of its mouth. It can then safely open its mouth to catch more.

ACTUAL SIZE

USE YOUR EYES

Use your eyes to study these zooms of birds that appear throughout the chapter. Can you recognize any of them just by looking at them? Are there any clues, such as color, body parts, or shape, that help you figure out where you've seen these images before?

1 I look like I've been dipped in paint.

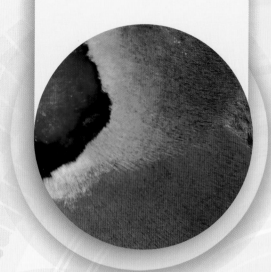

2 Shhh, I've got my eyes on you. I'm a silent hunter, so you won't hear me coming.

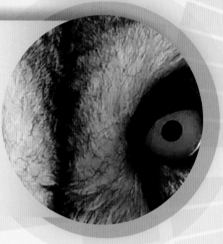

3 I spread my enormous wings and swoop over water.

4 I have brown plumage, but a white tail.

5 What yellow bird has been busy weaving this nest?

6 Two can see better than one, but one can see you!

7 I fly so fast I'm just a beautiful blue blur.

8 I am smart, I can talk, and I am handsome, too.

9 Welcome to the world, baby bird!

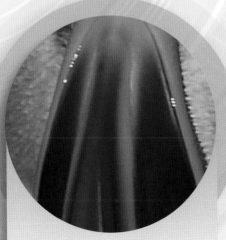

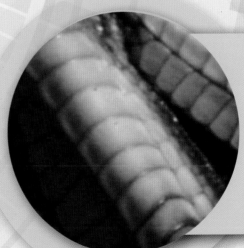

11 Who wants neat feet when they are wading through mud? I like my big feet, but who am I?

10 They say I look like a clown or a parrot. Do you agree?

OCEAN
LIFE

FEEDING THE OCEAN

Plankton are tiny sea creatures that provide food for the ocean's wildlife. They may be small, but they exist in billions. Plankton are eaten by fish and other ocean-dwelling creatures, and are at the bottom of the **food chain**. Most plankton live near the surface of the ocean, where there is light and warmth. Antarctic krill, however, are tough little creatures.

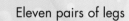

Large eyes help krill see in deep, dark water.

Eleven pairs of legs

Little and Large

See a krill up close and you can make out its tough outer skin, sensory antennae, and the special feeding limbs that filter microscopic food from the water. Most Antarctic krill are no larger than your little finger, yet these creatures live in vast swarms and are the main food for the largest animal that has ever lived—the blue whale.

ZOOM
x25

Transparent
body—light
passes through

Sit or Swim

This tiny animal, called an obelia, has a strange lifecycle. It spends part of its life attached to the seabed, and then reaches this jellyfish stage, called a medusa, and can swim. It may become food for other, larger animals.

ZOOM x100

Tough outer skin,
called a carapace

Krill

ZOOM x6

FACTOID

Krill can live in deep water, 2.5 miles (4 kilometers) below the surface, where there is no light and the water pressure would crush human bones.

VITAL STATISTICS

Common name	Antarctic krill
Latin name	*Euphausia superba*
Size	5.5 in (14 cm) in length
Habitat	Throughout oceans
Special feature	Feed on tiny plants

Amazing plankton

This radiolarian is a type of plankton. Most radiolarians are too small to be seen with the naked eye. This one lived many millions of years ago and has been fossilized—turned to stone—over time.

MARINE MARVELS

Life began in the oceans around 3.5 billion years ago. Look closely into a tide pool at the beach, and you will begin to get an idea of the huge range of living things that still rely on the oceans for life. When you zoom in on them, you will discover strange, dramatic, incredible lives unfolding.

◀ At low tide a huge variety of living things becomes visible in tide pools, lurking between stones and in the mud.

ZOOM x3

Star of the Ocean
Starfish belong to a group of animals called **echinoderms**. *They usually have five arms, and their mouth is in the center of their body, on the underside. A starfish's arms are equipped with hundreds of tiny "tube feet" with suckers (above). They are filled with liquid and move in waves, so the starfish can walk along the seabed.*

Caring for Eggs

This tiny sea horse has just hatched from its egg. When a female sea horse lays her eggs, the male scoops them up and keeps them in a special pouch. The eggs grow there until they are ready to hatch, so they are kept safe from predators.

ZOOM x30

Catching a Ride

Goose barnacles are animals that attach themselves to rocks and feed on plankton. A long time ago it was thought they grew into geese, which is how they got their strange name.

ZOOM x1.5

Spiky Stones

Sea urchins look like spiky stones and are a type of echinoderm. They often have venom (poison) in their spines and in their mouth, which is on their bottom! Some tropical urchins have spines that are 0.4 inches (one centimeter) thick.

ACTUAL SIZE

WHAT IS IT?

ZOOM x3

FLOWERY FIENDS

Jewel anemones look like beautiful underwater flowers, but they are poisonous predators. When clusters of jewel anemones live on the seabed or on rocks, they create a carpet of brightly colored animals. They range in color from pink to blue and green, but their good looks hide a deadly secret.

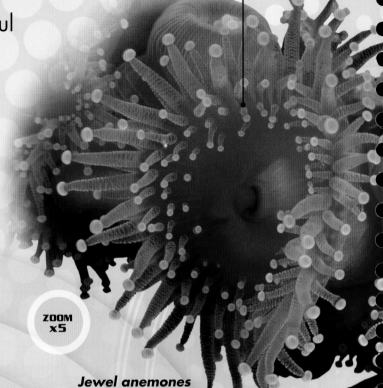

Three rings of tentacles

ZOOM x5

Jewel anemones

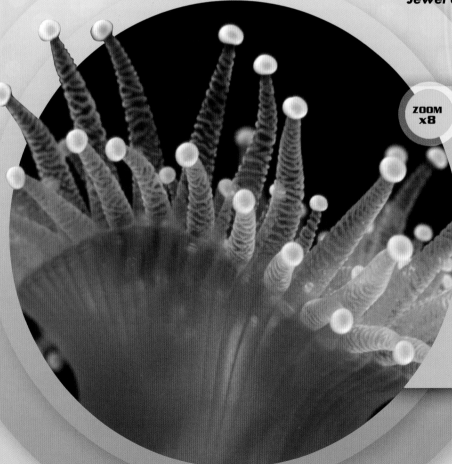

ZOOM x8

Hidden Weapons

This beautiful jewel anemone has stings in its stubby tentacles. When fish or other animals swim through the tentacles, the stings are fired at the prey, injecting painful venom. Some anemones have stings that work like harpoons, catching and dragging the prey to the animal's mouth.

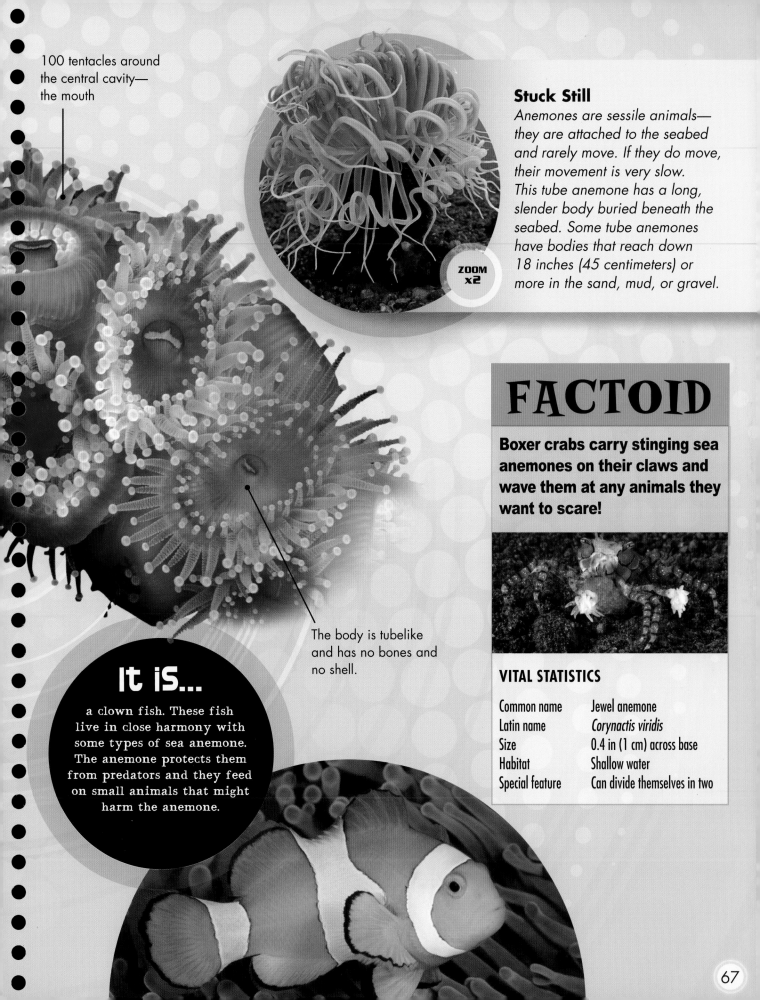

100 tentacles around the central cavity—the mouth

Stuck Still

Anemones are sessile animals—they are attached to the seabed and rarely move. If they do move, their movement is very slow. This tube anemone has a long, slender body buried beneath the seabed. Some tube anemones have bodies that reach down 18 inches (45 centimeters) or more in the sand, mud, or gravel.

ZOOM x2

The body is tubelike and has no bones and no shell.

It is...

a clown fish. These fish live in close harmony with some types of sea anemone. The anemone protects them from predators and they feed on small animals that might harm the anemone.

FACTOID

Boxer crabs carry stinging sea anemones on their claws and wave them at any animals they want to scare!

VITAL STATISTICS

Common name	Jewel anemone
Latin name	*Corynactis viridis*
Size	0.4 in (1 cm) across base
Habitat	Shallow water
Special feature	Can divide themselves in two

FANTASTIC FISH

What is a fish? There are so many types, in so many shapes, sizes, and colors, that it is hard to say exactly what makes a fish. The tiniest ocean fish are smaller than your fingernail, but the largest ones —whale sharks—grow to be up to 46 feet (14 meters) long.

ZOOM x88

◄ When a shark's skin is magnified, its extraordinary structure becomes visible. Each of these pointed scales is called a denticle and is more similar to a tooth than to an ordinary fish scale.

WHAT IS it?

Baby Fish

Few fish take care of their eggs or young. A brown trout female can lay 10,000 eggs at a time, in the hope that a few baby fish—called **fry**—make it to adulthood. Eggs and fry are a tasty, nutritious food for many other marine animals.

ZOOM
x30

Big Eyes

When divers swim up close to glasseye snappers, they get an eyeful. These nighttime hunters are fish with superb vision, thanks to their huge eyes. They can grow to be up to 20 inches (50 centimeters) long and live around reefs.

Deep Breathing

Seawater contains **oxygen**—the gas that fish breathe to release energy from food. Water goes into a fish's mouth and flows over its **gills**, which are located behind its head. This image of gills has been magnified to show how they have a large surface area to maximize the movement of oxygen into the fish's blood. A waste gas, carbon dioxide, passes out from the gills.

ZOOM
x250

WARNING STRIPES

When deepsea photographers want to take snaps of a lionfish, they are more likely to zoom out than zoom in! These good-looking fish don't wear their stripes for fun—they send out a clear signal that warns other animals to stay away, because those spines can hurt.

The dorsal fins carry venom, or poison.

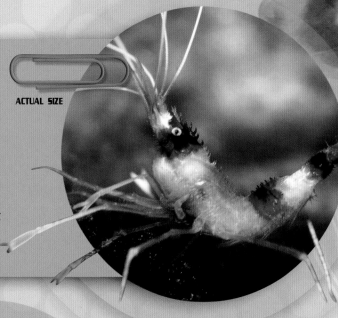

ACTUAL SIZE

Small and Spiky

The red stripes on a banded coral shrimp may help this little **crustacean** *hide, or they may warn hungry lionfish that the shrimp has a surprise in store. Look closely at its back and you will notice a row of sharp spines.*

Red-and-white stripes are a warning to predators to stay away.

It is...

a mackerel. The smooth scales on its shiny body reflect light. When a shoal of thousands of mackerel dart through the ocean, they create a bright sheet of shimmering light, which confuses their predators.

Fins on the side of the body—pectoral fins—are used to trap prey against rocks or coral.

Lionfish

Some sharks prey on lionfish —the stinging spines have no bad effects on them.

VITAL STATISTICS

Common name	Lionfish
Latin name	*Pterois*
Size	16 in (40 cm) in length
Habitat	Coastal waters in warm regions
Special feature	Venomous spines

ZOOM x15

Can You See Me?

A tiny anemone shrimp is easy to miss. It has an almost transparent body, which means it can hide itself between an anemone's tentacles, or among this white coral. When you are small and defenseless, it is a good idea to use your appearance to blend in, or disappear from view —and you just might avoid being eaten by something larger.

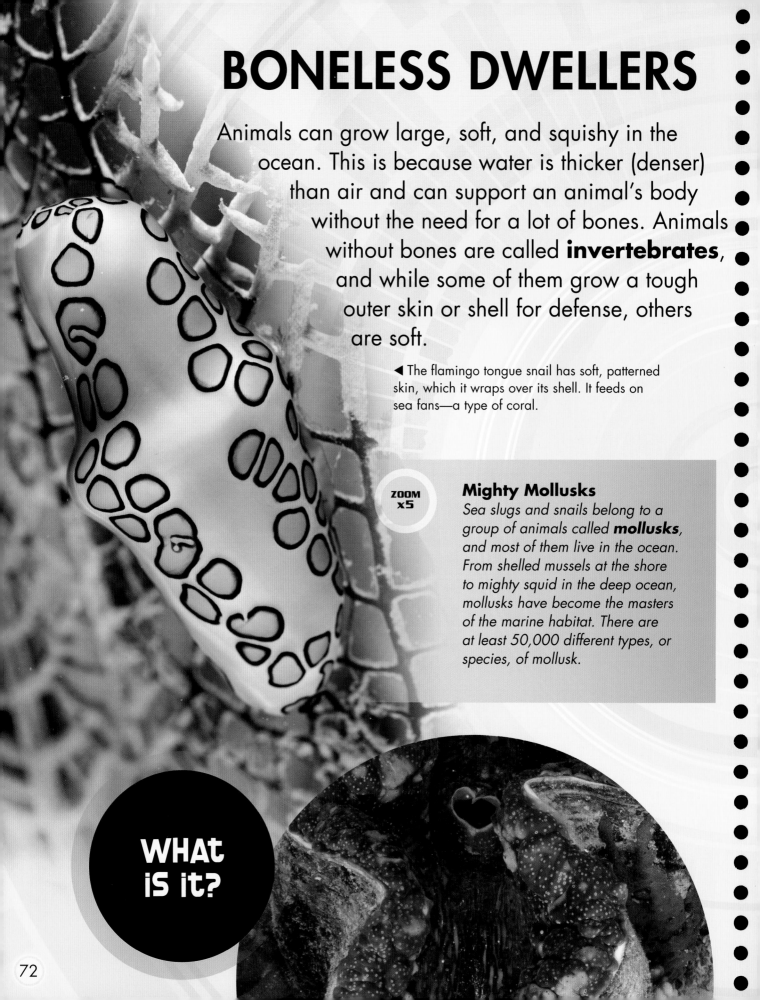

BONELESS DWELLERS

Animals can grow large, soft, and squishy in the ocean. This is because water is thicker (denser) than air and can support an animal's body without the need for a lot of bones. Animals without bones are called **invertebrates**, and while some of them grow a tough outer skin or shell for defense, others are soft.

◄ The flamingo tongue snail has soft, patterned skin, which it wraps over its shell. It feeds on sea fans—a type of coral.

ZOOM x5

Mighty Mollusks

*Sea slugs and snails belong to a group of animals called **mollusks**, and most of them live in the ocean. From shelled mussels at the shore to mighty squid in the deep ocean, mollusks have become the masters of the marine habitat. There are at least 50,000 different types, or species, of mollusk.*

WHAT IS IT?

Record Breaker

The longest animal ever found was a bootlace worm measuring 180 feet (55 meters) in length. This ragworm grows to be a mere 16 inches (40 centimeters), but it looks fearsome when magnified. It has four small eyes and two clusters of four tentacles on either side of its head.

Spectacular Spiral

This colorful spiral is part of a marine worm called a Christmas tree worm. Most of its body is out of view, enclosed by a shell-like tube. This spiral is an **organ** with two jobs—it operates like gills, allowing the worm to breathe, and it captures small particles of food that drift by.

ZOOM x8

ZOOM x2

ACTUAL SIZE

Deadly Venom

Cone shells look harmless, but they fire a harpoon loaded with venom that is powerful enough to stun and kill a person. Scientists who study the venom from these marine snails hope to use it to produce painkilling medicines.

SMALL BUT DEADLY

A blue-ringed octopus may be small, but it is deadly—with a "hazard" warning sign to match. Zoom in close and look at those bold blue rings. They show that the octopus is feeling threatened, and is ready to attack. Its saliva, or spit, contains fast-acting venom that can kill.

Blue-ringed octopus

Yellow or light-brown skin

Toxic Spike

Zoom up as close as you like to a deadly stonefish, but it may still be invisible. This camouflaged fish is one of the most venomous animals in the world. If you step on one of 13 spines on its back you could be injected with venom that causes excruciating pain, and even death.

It is...

a giant clam. These mollusks are up to 60 inches (150 centimeters) in length, and do not move from the seabed. They filter small particles of food from seawater and live in the shallow waters of the Pacific Ocean.

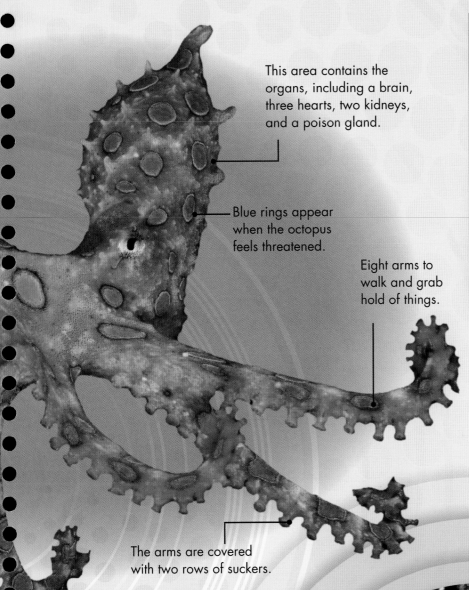

This area contains the organs, including a brain, three hearts, two kidneys, and a poison gland.

Blue rings appear when the octopus feels threatened.

Eight arms to walk and grab hold of things.

The arms are covered with two rows of suckers.

This octopus has a painless bite, but it has enough venom to paralyze ten adult humans.

VITAL STATISTICS

Common name	Blue-ringed octopus
Latin name	*Hapalochlaena*
Size	8 in (20 cm) in length
Habitat	Tropical areas of Pacific and Indian oceans
Special feature	Bright blue "warning" rings

ACTUAL SIZE

Feast or Famine?

Blue-ringed octopuses feast on fish, shrimp, and crabs. They bite their victim, or release poisonous saliva into the water around it. The octopus waits for the venom to take effect, then eats the prey. This mother octopus will not eat for six months while she protects her white, oval-shaped eggs. When they hatch, she will die.

COLORFUL CORAL

Coral reefs are often called rainforests of the ocean. They are special because they are home to around one quarter of all types of ocean-dwelling animals. Reefs are stony structures built by the tiny animals, called polyps, that live inside them.

◀ A coral polyp is closely related to a sea anemone. Like anemones, these small animals have a column-shaped body and rows of tentacles arranged around the mouth.

ZOOM x7

Super Stars
Coral reefs grow over thousands of years, and create a home, or habitat, for other creatures. This small brittle star uses its five arms to walk on the seafloor, but it can quickly scuttle into crevices in a reef if it is threatened.

ZOOM x10

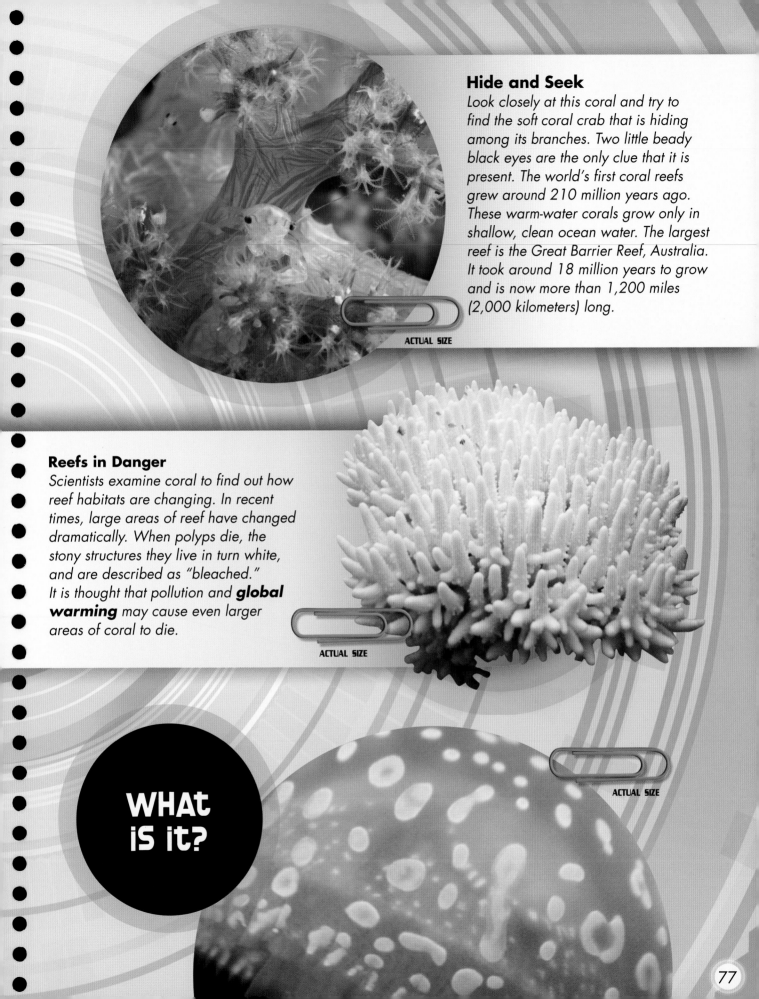

Hide and Seek

Look closely at this coral and try to find the soft coral crab that is hiding among its branches. Two little beady black eyes are the only clue that it is present. The world's first coral reefs grew around 210 million years ago. These warm-water corals grow only in shallow, clean ocean water. The largest reef is the Great Barrier Reef, Australia. It took around 18 million years to grow and is now more than 1,200 miles (2,000 kilometers) long.

ACTUAL SIZE

Reefs in Danger

*Scientists examine coral to find out how reef habitats are changing. In recent times, large areas of reef have changed dramatically. When polyps die, the stony structures they live in turn white, and are described as "bleached." It is thought that pollution and **global warming** may cause even larger areas of coral to die.*

ACTUAL SIZE

ACTUAL SIZE

WHAt iS it?

HUNTING FOR A HOME

Little hermit crabs are a coral reef's cleanup crew. They scuttle over rocky surfaces, picking up little pieces of food to nibble. This helps the coral polyps grow and stay healthy. Zoom in close to get a good look at this creature's extraordinary features.

ACTUAL SIZE

Jointed legs for walking and swimming

Hermit crab

ZOOM x20

FACTOID

Many crabs are scavengers and feed on dead animals. They also hunt, and may lose a claw in a battle. Fortunately, crabs can grow new legs to replace those they lose.

VITAL STATISTICS

Common name	Scarlet reef hermit crab
Latin name	*Paguristes cadenati*
Size	1.5 in (4 cm) legspan
Habitat	Coral reefs
Special feature	Live in a borrowed shell

Time to Grow
This is one of thousands of eggs laid by the horseshoe crab. The larva is growing inside, and it will take up to ten years for this animal to become an adult.

Eyes are on stalks.

Sensitive antennae for touch and to sense chemicals in the water or air.

A pair of strong claws

All Change

When crab larvae hatch from their eggs they look nothing like their tough-skinned, long-limbed parents. This little crab larva will swim with other plankton and feed by trapping food in its bristles. As it grows, it will sink to the seabed and remain hidden while its hard skin develops.

ZOOM x60

It is...

a spotted jellyfish that lives in the South Pacific. These animals are related to coral polyps, and have stinging tentacles. They are weak swimmers, and are carried along by ocean currents.

DEEP-SEA MONSTERS

The deeper you dive into the oceans, the darker it gets. At depths of around 650 feet (200 meters), little light can filter through, and at depths of 3,300 feet (1,000 meters), the ocean is inky-black. Zoom down into the deepest ocean zones and you'll find some of the world's most bizarre animals.

ACTUAL SIZE

◄ A young glass squid is called a larva and lives near the ocean's surface with other plankton. This adult, however, survives in deep, dark water to depths of 9,200 feet (2,800 meters).

Red Jelly
Ocean explorers use robots and remotely operated vehicles (ROVs) to dive down into the deepest places. They have discovered extraordinary animals, such as this small red jellyfish with its thousands of tentacles.

ZOOM x2

Under Pressure

ZOOM x2

Water is 850 times denser than air, which means it is very heavy. This hatchet fish lives in deep oceans and it has to cope with the enormous pressure exerted on its body by the weight of water above it. Every night, however, it swims up around 3,300 feet (1,000 meters) to feed on plankton at the ocean's surface.

ACTUAL SIZE

Ocean Hotspots

In the deep ocean, there are cracks on the seabed where heat from the inside of the planet escapes. They are called hydrothermal vents, and weird animals live here that can survive nowhere else on Earth, such as these giant tube worms (above).

WHAT IS IT?

BRIGHT LIGHTS

The deep ocean contains many mysteries, but marine scientists are discovering new animals all the time. One of the most incredible discoveries is the viperfish. These are powerful, fierce predators with a body that is perfectly suited to their deep-sea habitat.

ACTUAL SIZE

Large head

Long, thin, and very sharp fangs

Lines of photophores on the underside

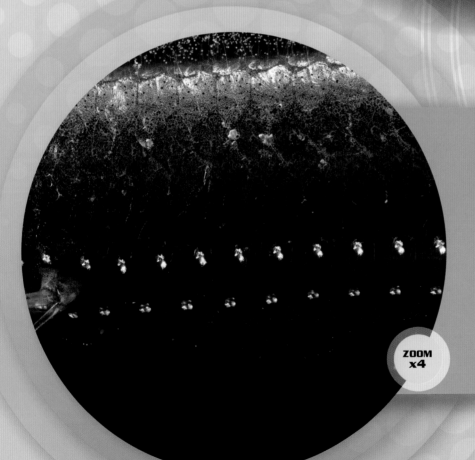

ZOOM x4

Glowing in the Dark

*Who needs the Sun's light when you can make your own? Some deep-water animals, including viperfish, have special organs in their body, called **photophores**, which make light. These help confuse predators, or attract prey and mates.*

The lure contains photophores and attracts prey.

Long, thin body

Viperfish

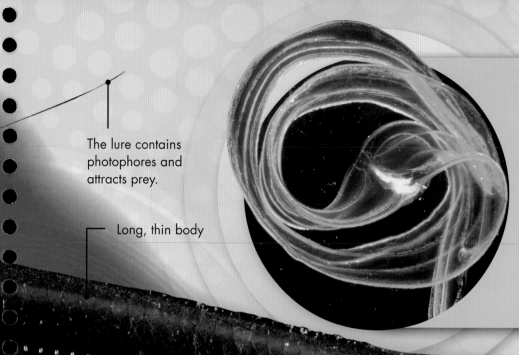

Glowing Ribbons

This strange-looking animal is called a comb jelly. Its ribbonlike body is covered on one side with tiny hairs, called cilia. Known as Venus's girdle, this animal swims with a snakelike movement and glows greenish-gold at night.

FACTOID

A female hatchet fish is large, but her partner is tiny. He stays stuck to her body, feeding off her, and fertilizing her eggs.

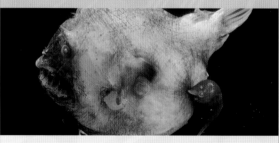

VITAL STATISTICS

Common name	Viperfish
Latin name	*Chauliodus* species
Size	12 in (30 cm) in length
Habitat	At depths of 3,300 ft (1,000 m)
Special feature	Can make its own light

It is...

a deep-water dumbo octopus. Its tentacles are covered with small bristles called cirri. When the cirri move backward and forward, they create water currents that drag food into the octopus's mouth.

USE YOUR EYES

Use your eyes to study these zooms that appear throughout the chapter. Can you recognize any of the animals just by looking at these pictures? Are there any clues, such as color or shape, that help you work out where you've seen these images before?

1 *I am too soft to survive, so I borrow someone else's home.*

2 *I have a long journey to find food, but my body is up to the challenge.*

3 *I'm small but deadly, so beware my rings of blue.*

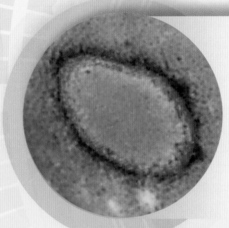

4 *I walk with my arms. How strange is that?*

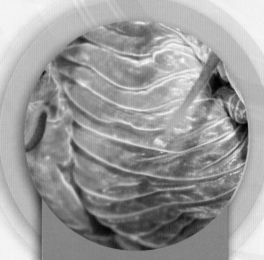

5 *My cousins can grow up to 180 feet (55 meters), but I'm just as fearsome!*

6 Which "fish" has both arms and feet? That's me!

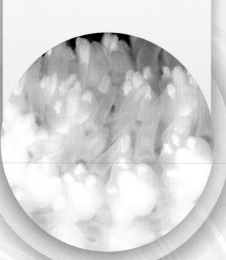

7 I have a bad temper and spines to match. Divers beware!

8 Giant blue whales make a meal of me.

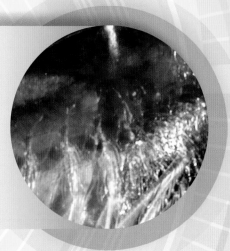

9 I am named after a large water bird, but I can't fly anywhere.

10 My cousins are slugs and snails— would you believe it?

11 If you see my fangs, you are in deep water!

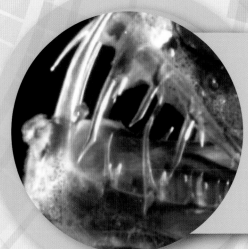

Answers: 1. p78 2. p81 3. p74-75 4. p76 5. p73 6. p64 7. p70-71 8. p62-63 9. p65 10. p72 11. p82

PLANTS

ENERGY MACHINES

We need plants because they take the energy in sunlight and convert it into food. It is a process called **photosynthesis**. While they are performing this fabulous feat, plants make oxygen, which is the gas we use to turn food back into energy. So, without plants, we could neither eat nor breathe!

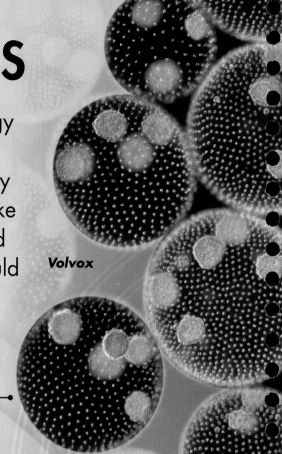

Volvox

Each Volvox is just one cell.

The colony is held inside a jellylike wall.

ZOOM x100

The Smallest Plants
Living things are made up of building blocks called cells. Huge trees are made of billions of cells, but the simplest plants, such as Volvox, are just one cell. These plants are called **algae** *(say: al-gee), and they live in water. Millions of strands of the algae Spirogyra (left) create slimy, green pond scum.*

ZOOM x130

One or two hairlike tails, called flagella, make the colony move.

Green algae (they contain chlorophyll)

The Cycle of Life

Tiny one-celled animals called rotifers (below) eat Volvox, and baby fish eat rotifers. Larger fish, tadpoles, and birds all eat baby fish—and so the Sun's energy moves along a chain of living things.

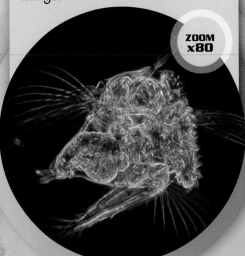

ZOOM x80

FACTOID

Seaweeds are algae. They are used to make medicines and foods, such as ice cream.

VITAL STATISTICS

Common name	Red algae
Latin name	*Antithamnion plumula*
Size	2 in (5 cm) in length
Habitat	Rocky shores
Special feature	Each strand is one cell thick

Small but mighty

*Diatoms look like nothing else on Earth. They are tiny algae that use a tough substance called **silica** to make their cell walls extra strong. Most diatoms live in seas and oceans.*

TOWERS AND TUBES

Plants have important jobs to do. They position themselves to grab as much sunshine as possible, so they can photosynthesize and grow. They collect water from the soil, make food, and move **nutrients** around. When you zoom inside a plant you can see exactly how it is able to carry out these essential tasks.

ACTUAL SIZE

Super Highways

Stems work like strong but flexible towers, raising the leaves away from the soil so they can reach more light. They connect the food production areas—the leaves—with the plant's roots, flowers, and fruits. Nutrients such as minerals, food, and water travel along them.

ZOOM x800

WHAT IS it?

Inside Stems

Long tubes run the length of the stems. Some tubes carry water from the roots to the plant. They are called xylem vessels. Others carry food, mostly in the form of sugar, around the plant. They are called phloem tubes (say: flo-em).

ZOOM x90

Flexible Bamboo

Air spaces between the cells keep the stem strong, but light and flexible. Bamboo stems have large hollow centers, and some types can grow to be up to 100 feet (30 meters) in height.

ZOOM x80

Staying Strong

Simple plant cells are packed together like boxes. Each cell has **cellulose** in its walls, to make the plant strong. The dark area in a cell is the nucleus—it is the plant's control center.

ZOOM x260

91

MOSS MOUNTAINS

Some of our planet's most amazing plants are ones we walk on, or over, without even noticing them. Mosses, for example, look just like bouncy green cushions—until you zoom in on them. They can grow to be several feet wide, or may be so small they can be seen only with a microscope.

Spore capsules fire spores into the air.

The leaves collect water.

FACTOID

Mosses have been around for about 300 million years, and there are more than 12,000 species, or types.

VITAL STATISTICS

Common name	Marsh moss
Latin name	*Sphagnum*
Size	1.6 in (4 cm) in height
Habitat	Wet places
Special feature	Can hold a lot of water in its structure

It is...

a water bear or moss piglet, and it hides in moss. It looks fearsome, but it's tiny: this image is magnified 220 times. If it dries out, a water bear can survive for ten years, frozen in time until it gets wet again.

Lighter than Air
Tiny moss **spores** have a tough outer coat to protect them. They are so small and light they can float away on the gentlest breeze.

ZOOM x1000

ZOOM x2

Moss

Exploding Plants
The first plants that grew on land had no flowers or seeds. Today's mosses, **liverworts**, and **ferns** are related to those early plants, and they also produce spores instead of seeds. Zoom into this moss and you can see tall stalks, called sporophytes. Each capsule at the top of a sporophyte holds thousands of spores.

ZOOM x10

TALENTED TREES

Conifers are record-breaking plants. They are the tallest, smallest, and oldest trees. Bonsai cypress trees and shore pines reach only 8 inches (20 centimeters) in height. Redwoods, by contrast, reach heights of 310 feet (95 meters), and one tree weighs ten times more than a blue whale. They grow from tiny seeds less than a quarter inch (5 millimeters) across.

◄ Dwarf conifers never grow taller than 3 feet (1 meter).

Extreme Survivors

Many conifers can thrive in extreme habitats. Freezing winds and snow suit conifers in the far north, while those in dry places can endure months with no rain. Some Californian bristlecone pines have survived for 5,000 years—and were hundreds of years old when the ancient Egyptians built the pyramids.

ACTUAL SIZE

ZOOM x6

WHAT IS IT?

Saving Water

Conifer leaves are usually shaped like needles or scales, and have a waxy layer on the outside. This helps them save water and survive in cold weather. Most conifers are evergreen, which means they don't lose their leaves each year.

Magic Numbers

Pinecone scales are arranged in two sets of spirals—one counterclockwise and one clockwise. The number of spirals follows a unique mathematical sequence of numbers, called the **Fibonacci series**. It is the best way to pack in a lot of scales evenly and without gaps.

ACTUAL SIZE

ZOOM x3

ZOOM x2

Cones and Seeds

One conifer tree grows both male and female cones. The yellow pollen on these little male cones will be carried, by wind, to the larger female cones. The pollen fertilizes their eggs, but it takes up to three years for a female cone to mature. Once the seeds are grown, they fall to the ground.

FANCY FLOWERS

Trek through a rainforest and you will be surrounded by green. Huge emerald leaves, dangling green creepers, and frilly fern fronds fill every space. Then your eye will catch the dazzling display of flowers, nestled in the crook of a tree. Showy, colorful, and scented—flowers put on a bold display for a reason.

Orchid

ZOOM x2

Big Flower or Little Flowers?

How big is a sunflower flower? You might think it is as big as your hand, or even bigger. Zoom in, and you will see that one sunflower head actually contains hundreds of flowers, each called a **floret** *and no larger than your fingernail. Each floret produces one seed.*

ACTUAL SIZE

One petal, shaped like a landing platform, leads the insect toward the **nectary**.

It is...

a bee orchid. These flowers look and smell like female bees. When male bees try to mate with the flower, pollen rubs off on their back, from which they accidentally transfer it to other flowers.

Sugary liquid is produced in the nectary to attract insects.

Bright, colorful petals attract insects.

Pollen is carried on stamens. It gets brushed onto insects that pass by.

The **stigma** is connected to the ovary, which contains a flower's eggs.

FACTOID

The world's largest flowers are Rafflesias, and they stink like rotting meat. One flower can measure 3 feet (90 centimeters) in width.

VITAL STATISTICS

Common name	Orchid
Latin name	*Family Orchidaceae*
Size	100 in (2.5 m) in height
Habitat	Mostly in warm, damp places
Special feature	Beautiful flowers

ZOOM x3

Secrets Inside

*Scientists zoom into a plant's insides to understand how it reproduces. This flower has been cut in half, lengthwise, to reveal its hidden reproductive organs. Long, pollen-tipped **stamens** surround the carpel, which protects the tiny round eggs that are nestling inside its fleshy tissues.*

PLANTS ON THE MOVE

When animals want to mate, it's easy. They can walk, swim, or fly to find the perfect partner. Plants, however, are usually rooted to the ground. They overcome this problem by sending tiny parts of themselves—pollen—out into the world.

ZOOM x5

◄ Tiny granules of orange pollen coat the **anthers** of a lily flower. The anthers are the top part of a stamen.

What is Pollen?

Pollen contains male sex cells, which combine with female sex cells, or eggs, to make seeds. When pollen lands on a stigma—the female part of a flower—**pollination** has taken place. The pollen grows a tube down the stigma to reach the ovary, and then combines with an egg inside. This is called fertilization.

Tough Travelers

Some pollen grains are ribbed, or spiked; others are round, oval, flat, or plump. It all depends on which plant they come from. The outer wall of a pollen grain is so tough it can survive for tens of thousands of years. One flower may produce thousands of pollen grains.

ZOOM x1000

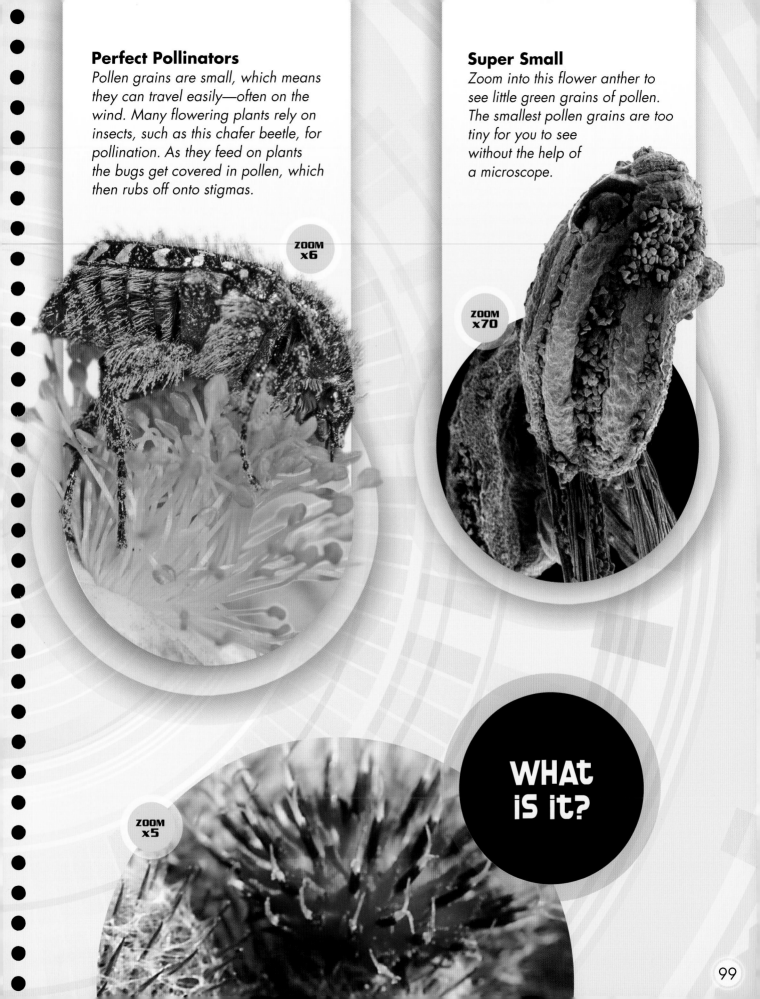

Perfect Pollinators

Pollen grains are small, which means they can travel easily—often on the wind. Many flowering plants rely on insects, such as this chafer beetle, for pollination. As they feed on plants the bugs get covered in pollen, which then rubs off onto stigmas.

ZOOM x6

Super Small

Zoom into this flower anther to see little green grains of pollen. The smallest pollen grains are too tiny for you to see without the help of a microscope.

ZOOM x70

ZOOM x5

WHAT IS IT?

SEED JOURNEYS

Plants do not make caring parents. Once they have produced their seeds, most plants want their offspring to go as far away as possible! They don't want to be fighting for space, light, and water. So they produce seeds that are well equipped to go on a long journey— by one means or another!

The pappus lifts the seed up in wind.

Each seed is attached so lightly to the plant that the smallest breeze will lift it up.

FACTOID

According to folklore, the number of puffs it takes to blow all the seeds off a dandelion seedhead tells you the time of day. Four puffs means it is four o'clock in the afternoon.

VITAL STATISTICS

Common name	Dandelion
Latin name	*Taraxacum officinale*
Size	7 in (17.5 cm) in height
Habitat	Grassland and wasteland
Special feature	Each flowerhead can have more than 150 florets

ZOOM x2.5

Juicy Fruits
After fertilization, some ovaries grow into fruits, or berries. Animals eat the fruits, and the seeds inside pass through their body, coming out in their feces (say: fee-sees). In the right conditions, the seeds will germinate and grow into new plants.

Dandelion

ZOOM x3

New Beginnings

*When a seed has the right conditions of water, soil, and temperature, it may begin to grow a root, and eventually develop into a new plant. This is called **germination**.*

ZOOM x6

The fine hairs are called the pappus.

It is...

a burdock flower. Seeds develop inside the tough capsules, or burrs. Little hooks on a burr attach it to a passing animal, or person, and it is carried to a new place where the seeds may have the right conditions to grow.

GREEN DEFENDERS

Many animals, including us, know that plants can make tasty, healthy food. To survive, plants have some clever ways of defending themselves. Red yew berries look tasty but are poisonous to some animals, and hard nuts are impossible for all but the strongest beaks to break.

Prickly Plant

The peculiar shape of a cactus helps this prickly plant cope in a challenging environment. Sharp spines cover large green pads that look like giant leaves. In fact, the spines are leaves, and the pads are swollen stems. The stems store water—essential in a dry habitat where it rarely rains.

Sharp and Cutting

Spines, spikes, prickles, and thorns are a first line of defense for many plants. It would take a brave animal to place its jaws around a hairy mary plant. Each stem is smothered in needle-pointed spines, measuring up to 3 inches (7.5 centimeters) in length.

ACTUAL SIZE

Transferring Poison

Milkweed produces toxic (poisonous) juice, or sap, which is deadly to most insects. Monarch caterpillars, however, eat the plant and store the deadly chemicals in their own body, making them poisonous to the animals that feed on them.

ZOOM x3

Toxic Ooze

Storing poisonous chemicals in a plant's tissues is another crafty way to deter hungry creatures. Rubber trees make sticky latex. It is toxic, but also traps insects trying to feed on the tree.

Plant Attack

Hairs on a nettle leaf are tipped with tiny beads of silica (left). If you brush against the leaf, the tips will snap off and the hairs will spear your skin, injecting foul chemicals. One chemical causes pain, while another makes the skin swollen, red, and itchy. Even grasses contain sharp pieces of silica.

ZOOM x 100

WHAT IS IT?

ZOOM x4

MEAT-EATING PLANTS

When you look closely at plants, you begin to discover that they hold some strange but deadly secrets. In the endless battle for survival, animals usually turn plants into food—but in some rare cases, plants are the winners because they actually eat animals!

Red color and sweet-smelling nectar attract insects.

FACTOID

Small flies can escape from the traps. This means the plant spends time and energy only on digesting larger meaty meals.

VITAL STATISTICS

Common name	Venus flytrap
Latin name	*Dionaea muscipula*
Size	Leaves are 12 in (30 cm) in length
Habitat	Damp, mossy places
Special feature	The traps are closed for up to ten days, while a bug is digested

ZOOM x2

Extreme Measures
The leaves of pitcher plants form colorful cups to attract insects. Curious bugs fall into the cups, which contain a mixture of water and flesh-dissolving chemicals.

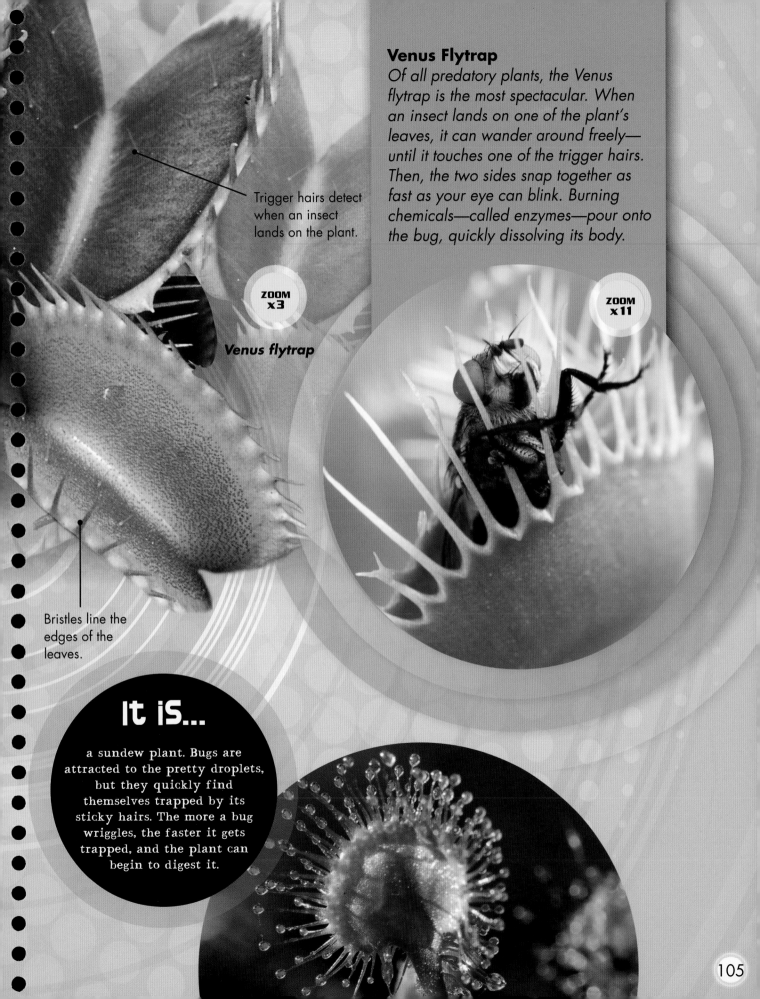

Trigger hairs detect when an insect lands on the plant.

Venus Flytrap

Of all predatory plants, the Venus flytrap is the most spectacular. When an insect lands on one of the plant's leaves, it can wander around freely—until it touches one of the trigger hairs. Then, the two sides snap together as fast as your eye can blink. Burning chemicals—called enzymes—pour onto the bug, quickly dissolving its body.

ZOOM x3

Venus flytrap

ZOOM x11

Bristles line the edges of the leaves.

It is...

a sundew plant. Bugs are attracted to the pretty droplets, but they quickly find themselves trapped by its sticky hairs. The more a bug wriggles, the faster it gets trapped, and the plant can begin to digest it.

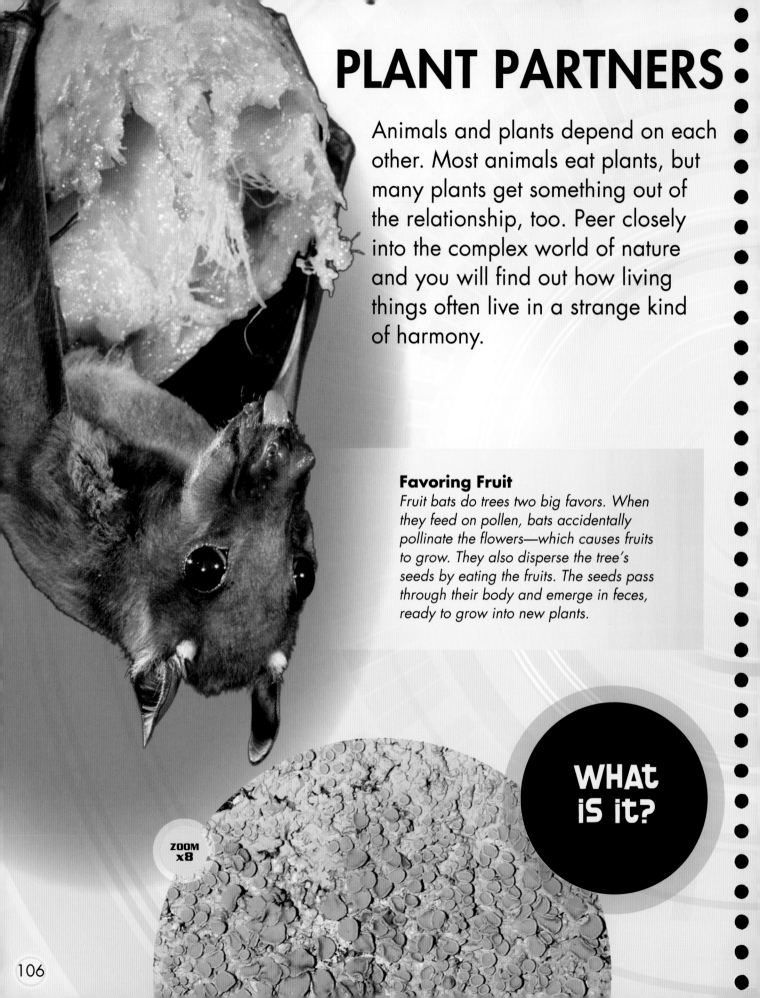

PLANT PARTNERS

Animals and plants depend on each other. Most animals eat plants, but many plants get something out of the relationship, too. Peer closely into the complex world of nature and you will find out how living things often live in a strange kind of harmony.

Favoring Fruit

Fruit bats do trees two big favors. When they feed on pollen, bats accidentally pollinate the flowers—which causes fruits to grow. They also disperse the tree's seeds by eating the fruits. The seeds pass through their body and emerge in feces, ready to grow into new plants.

ZOOM x8

WHAT IS it?

Tough Nuts

Agoutis are the only animals that can open the tough outer husk of a brazil nut. They have extremely strong incisor teeth, which keep growing throughout their lives. Brazil nut trees rely on agoutis to spread their seeds and if these rodents (which are endangered) died out, so would the trees.

Civet Coffee

Palm civets enjoy the taste of juicy berries that grow on coffee plants. The seeds are partly digested and passed out in feces, and may germinate. In a strange twist, the seeds—coffee beans—are collected by people to be ground up and used to brew a delicious type of coffee— the most expensive in the world.

ZOOM x10

Taking in Lodgers

Acacia trees love having ants to visit. Ants not only attack insect pests, they even destroy nearby plants that might take light or water from the acacia. In return, the tree rewards its ants by making little orange beads of food on its leaves. Ants feed the beads to their larvae (young).

FRUITING FUNGI

When is a plant not a plant? When it is a fungus. These strange living things lead a very different life from that of green plants. Instead of using light to make food, fungi feed on living things or the remains of dead things. Mushrooms, **mold**, and yeast are different types of fungus.

Fly agaric

ZOOM
x2

Going Underground
Fungi don't have roots. They have tiny feeding threads, called hyphae (say: hi-fee), which grow through soil, or the animal or plant they are feeding on. The hyphae absorb nutrients and can spread into dense networks that cover huge distances underground, making them the largest living things on Earth.

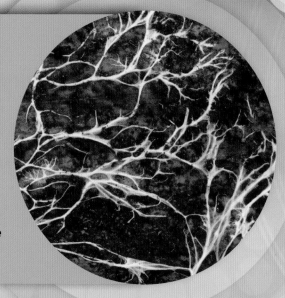

It is...
a lichen. Scientists once thought lichens were types of plant, until they zoomed in close and discovered that a lichen is actually made up of a fungus and an alga living together.

The cap protects the gills, where spores are produced.

Fly agaric is the white-spotted red toadstool that is often illustrated in fairytales and other picture books.

VITAL STATISTICS

Common name	Fly agaric
Latin name	*Amanita muscaria*
Size	4 in (10 cm) in length
Habitat	Under birch and spruce trees
Special feature	Poisonous and should NEVER be tasted

The fruiting body usually grows upward, so the spores can disperse.

Heads in the Air

The part of a fungus we can usually spot, such as a mushroom, is called the fruiting body. It makes millions of microscopic spores that drift in the air. Bracket fungi grow huge fruiting spores on trees and rotting wood. The tiniest fruiting bodies are often molds, and are microscopic in size.

ZOOM x3,000

USE YOUR EYES

Use your eyes to study these zooms that appear throughout the chapter. Can you recognize any of them just by looking at them? Are there any clues, such as color or shape, that help you work out where you've seen these images before?

1 *I am a super-strong alga with silica to toughen me up.*

2 *Isn't nature brilliant? Look how neatly I am packed together. But what am I?*

3 *We may be tiny but we are tough, and can survive long journeys. We often travel by insect!*

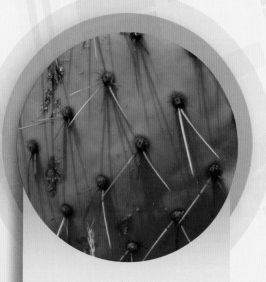

4 *Ouch! These prickly spines have an important job to do.*

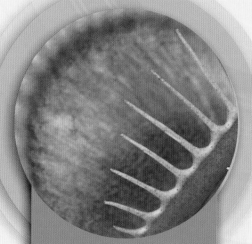

5 *Come close, we are snappy to see you!*

6 Small and tasty, we appeal to ants. What are we?

7 Huge needle-like spines cover my stems. I look scary!

8 I may be pretty but I hide a deep, dark secret. Do you know what I am?

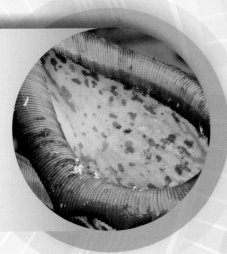

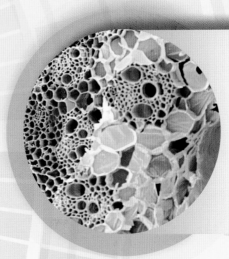

9 Cut me in half, take a super-thin slice, and put me under a microscope.

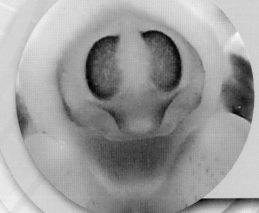

11 My good looks appeal to people, but I want to impress those beautiful bees.

10 Gently blow and use me to tell the time.

GLOSSARY

Algae Simple plants that photosynthesize, but do not have true stems and roots. Algae do not grow flowers. Seaweeds are algae.

Antennae Long, slender organs on an animal's head that help it sense what is going on around it. They can usually detect touch, smell, and taste.

Anther Part of a stamen that holds the pollen.

Barb A hairlike thread that grows from a feather's main shaft.

Barbule A tiny thread that grows from a barb.

Brood All of the eggs, or young, that are produced at one time.

Camouflage Colors or patterns that help an animal stay hidden from view.

Cell Living things are made up of cells, which are often described as the building blocks of organisms.

Cellulose A tough substance that lines the walls of plant cells, giving them strength and structure.

Cocoon The silken case spun by an insect to protect the pupa.

Colony A group of animals that live closely together.

Crest Many birds have decorative feathers on their head, which are known as crests. They may be used to impress mates.

Crustacean An animal with four or more pairs of limbs, a body that is divided into segments, and a tough exoskeleton. Most crustaceans live in water.

Cuticle The tough outer skin of a bug.

Digestive juice When an animal digests food, it breaks it down into smaller parts that can be absorbed into its body. Its body makes powerful liquids, called digestive juices or enzymes, to do this.

Downy Soft, fine, and fluffy. Downy feathers are ideal for keeping a bird warm.

Echinoderm A type of marine animal that is often circular in shape and has a symmetry of five. Sea urchins, starfish, and brittle stars are echinoderms.

Eyespot Some animals have patterns on their body that resemble the eyes of larger animals. These eyespots may help scare away predators.

Fern A plant with feathery fronds. They do not have flowers, and they produce spores rather than seeds.

Fertilize When a male sex cell joins with a female sex cell. After fertilization in plants, a seed may grow.

Fibonacci series A number series in which each number is the sum of the two numbers before it, for example, 1, 1, 2, 3, 5, 8, etc.

Floret A small flower that is one of many making up a flowerhead.

Food chain A chain of animals that depend on each other for food. Plants are normally at the bottom of a food chain; they are eaten by one animal, which is eaten by another animal, and so on.

Fry Baby fish. When they first hatch they are sometimes called larvae.

Gene Animal cells contain genes, which hold all the information necessary for the animal to live, grow, and reproduce.

Germination When a seed begins to grow.

Gills Organs that are used to take oxygen out of water, and to pass the waste gas (carbon dioxide) out of the body. Fish have gills.

Global warming The warming of Earth's atmosphere. This means the oceans are also getting hotter.

Grub Young, soft-bodied bugs are larvae, but they are also sometimes called grubs or maggots.

Invertebrate An animal that does not have a backbone. Mollusks, worms, and insects are invertebrates.

Iridescence Colors that seem to change when they are seen from different angles are described as iridescent.

Katydid A green or brown insect that belongs to the same family as crickets and grasshoppers.

Keratin A tough substance that is used in nature to make skin, nails, hair, scales, hooves, and feathers.

Larva (plural: larvae) A newly hatched animal. It will eventually change and grow into an adult.

Lens A transparent object with curved sides that gathers light and bends light rays. Lenses in eyes focus light rays into the back of the eye, so an animal can see. Lenses in cameras and microscopes are made of glass and can magnify an image.

Lifecycle The way an animal begins its life, grows, reproduces, and eventually dies.

Liverwort A simple plant with leaves that have lobes. Liverworts live in moist places and do not grow flowers.

Macro lens Used in a camera to take photographs close to the subject.

Mandible The mouthparts of a bug.

Mantis This insect is also known as a mantid, and is related to the cockroach.

Membrane A thin layer, like a sheet, that separates the inside parts of an animal's body or makes a lining around organs.

Metamorphosis The way a young bug, or larva, changes into an adult.

Mollusk An invertebrate with a soft body that usually lives in damp places or water habitats, such as the ocean. Snails, octopuses, shellfish, and squid are mollusks. Most mollusks grow shells.

Mold Fungi that are commonly found growing on food or decaying matter. They are very small organisms, but can grow into large colonies and cause disease.

Molt When a creature grows larger and sheds its old skin, or cuticle.

Nectary Part of a flower that produces a sweet liquid called nectar. Nectar attracts insects to the plant.

Nutrient A substance that, when taken in to the body, helps an organism live and grow.

Organ An area of the body, such as the brain, lung, or heart, that performs a special job.

Oxygen The gas that is produced by plants, and that animals breathe to live.

Photophore An organ that produces light.

Photosynthesis The process by which plants use the Sun's light to make food.

Pigment Chemicals that give an animal color.

Plume This is another word for a feather, especially one that is colorful or downy.

Pollen The yellow dust on a flower's stamens. Each pollen grain contains a single male sex cell. If it combines with a plant's egg, the egg is fertilized, and a seed can grow.

Pollination When pollen is transferred to the female part of a flower.

Proboscis A long, slender mouthpart through which some bugs absorb liquid.

Protein Essential substances that all living things need to grow, because cells are made of protein.

Pupa The stage of an insect's life cycle when it is going through the change from larva to adult. It is in a tough case, called a chrysalis, which protects it at this time.

Rachis The central shaft of a feather.

Scavenge A method of feeding that involves finding and eating any available food, including animals that have died.

Seed A plant's unit of reproduction. It can, in the right circumstances, grow into another plant.

Silica A tough mineral that occurs naturally in some plants.

Spiderling A young spider that has just hatched from its egg.

Spore The unit of reproduction for some simple plants, and fungi. Spores can, under the right circumstances, grow into plants.

Stamen The male part of a flower. It is made up of a filament that is topped by a pollen-coated anther.

Stigma The female part of a flower that receives the pollen during pollination.

Talons A bird of prey's powerful, clawed feet.

Tropical The "tropics" are a region of Earth near the Equator, between the Tropic of Cancer and the Tropic of Capricorn. Tropical areas have days and nights of similar length, and have hot climates.

Ultraviolet A type of light that cannot be seen by humans, but is visible to many other animals—especially insects.

Venom A type of poison that is made by animals and injected into another animal's body, often by biting or stinging.

Wingspan The measurement across both of a bird's outstretched wings. The measurement is taken from tip to tip.

INDEX

NOTES FOR PARENTS AND TEACHERS

Photography and microscopy are two uses of the physics of light and lenses can be applied to our everyday lives. Find some books in your local library or use the Internet* to track down diagrams that show how lenses bend (refract) light passing through them. Look at diagrams that show both convex and concave lenses, to discover how the shape of a lens changes the effect. Together, you can work out which of these two types of lens is used in microscopes, telescopes, and binoculars. You can also use the Internet to explore the role of lenses in the human eye, and how corrective lenses in eyeglasses are used to improve eyesight.

On a sunny day, you can demonstrate the focusing power of a lens. Hold a magnifying lens just above a piece of paper that is laid out in sunshine. Angle the lens until the light is focused on the paper, as a small bright dot. As it heats, the paper will smoke and burn. Make sure hair and clothing are kept well away from the paper as it could set them alight.

It is easy to make a water lens that shows how even a simple lens can magnify images. Lay a sheet of transparent plastic over a piece of newspaper text. Use a syringe or small spoon to place a single drop of water on the plastic. You will notice that the text beneath the water drop is magnified. Find out what happens when you make the drop larger, or smaller.

Take a walk to the park with some plastic containers, a magnifying glass, a pad of drawing paper, a ruler, and some pencils. See how many bugs you can collect in your containers. Look at them closely with the magnifying glass and make a list of them all. If you don't know the name of an insect, make a drawing of it or take its picture with a camera, and use a book or the Internet to identify it once you get home. Which ones have spots and which ones have wings? How many legs do they have? Do any have pincers? Which ones might be camouflaged? When looking at bugs make sure to be gentle so you don't harm them, and always put them back where you found them.

Take a walk outdoors and listen for bird song. Count how many different types of bird you can hear. Can you imitate the songs you hear? When you see a bird you can make a note of identifiers, such as size, color, tail length, and beak shape. While you are walking keep an eye out for any feathers on the ground. Bring them home and use them as the start of a bird-spotting scrapbook. At home, make a journal of bird song to learn at what times of the day they do most of their singing. Some birds are more active at night and others make the most noise in the morning. Also keep an ear out for the sound of baby birds in their nests. Why do you think they might be making such a racket? Do you know which birds these are? You can also zoom farther into the world of birds with a pair of binoculars and an identification book. This simple activity helps children learn the rewards of sitting quietly and observing.

Tide pools are a magnificent place to get a glimpse of what lives in our oceans and seas. Take a trip to the shore and try to find a small tide pool to observe. Collect stones, shells, and pieces of seaweed, and look at them closely. Once you have established that water bends light, encourage the child to experiment with the way an image can appear distorted when seen through water. Do the colors on a shell appear brighter or more muted when they are underwater? Discuss who might live in the shells and why they might be empty. Has a predator eaten what was inside? If you find any shells with animals still living in them, leave them where you found them—if there's an animal inside, it is somebody's home!

Photography underwater can be difficult. Talk about what those problems might be, and how they might be overcome. Use the Internet to investigate underwater cameras and how they work. Search for ROVs (remotely operated vehicles) and deep-water submersibles, such as *Alvin*, to discover how scientists and explorers have uncovered some of the ocean's deepest secrets.

Help children explore the ways we all use plants. Discuss how wheat seeds and yeast are used to make bread. Find out how cotton grows, and is turned into fabric. Identify how many ordinary items, such as pencils, paper, and yarn, are made from plant materials. Search your local park for any leaves, seeds, and nuts on the ground and take them home if you don't think any animals will mind. Discuss the difference between a nut, a seed, a flower, and a leaf. These can be traced around and the tracings can then be colored in. You can also take paper and pencils to a forest and make rubbings of the different tree barks. What is the purpose of bark and how does it protect trees?

Teach children to respect the wildlife around them. They can watch wildlife, visit the shore, and observe the world around them without harming it. Encourage them to understand that plants are often animals' habitats and food sources, and that animals and their homes must not be disturbed. When out walking make sure you set a good example by leaving the environment clean and pick up any garbage you might come across.

Discussing ways of protecting the environment is a good way to encourage children to appreciate the natural world. Also remind children that some plants, such as poison ivy, can sting or are poisonous, and some have thorns, so they should exercise care when out exploring.

Many naturalists discover a love of wildlife simply by observing animals, sketching, or photographing them, and making notes about their behavior.